Adam & Callie
  Wanted you to have
a book from the
first printing!
  Thanks for just
believing the ole'
gal could actually
do this!

　　　Love you
　　　both —
　　　Mom

The Patchwork of Our Lives

Peggy Foutch

authorHOUSE®

AuthorHouse™
1663 Liberty Drive
Bloomington, IN 47403
www.authorhouse.com
Phone: 1-800-839-8640

First published by AuthorHouse 3/8/2011

ISBN: 978-1-4567-3662-0 (e)
ISBN: 978-1-4567-3663-7 (sc)

Library of Congress Control Number: 2011902383

Printed in the United States of America

Dear Readers:

Thank you so much for choosing my book, I do hope it brings you enjoyment, and you will be eager to read the second book of this series, coming soon.

I want to take this opportunity to thank several people for their time and patience, and all the contributions of ideas and wisdom that was generated during this process. To Sue Ann for planting the seed, Barb, who from the beginning, encouraged me to elaborate, and keep going no matter what, thank you for all you did. Patty for some of her memories of grandma's house and belongings, Diane and Cheryl for reading and sharing ideas. Dr. Harley Foutch, for information of MTSU, and his daughter Michelle Rowe, for her knowledge in physical therapy. Aleta, there is no way to thank you for your time in reading, proofreading, and more proofreading, and your ideas. And especially thanks to my husband Tony, for his patience when I was working on the book and should have been cooking or cleaning. I thank you one and all.

Peggy

Chapter 1

Katie knew when she opened her eyes that it would all be a dream. If not, she was sure her heart was going to jump out of her chest. Someone was telling her to breathe. This just could not be real, could it? She felt as though she was going to faint, again. She couldn't seem to get enough air into her lungs. Her head was spinning; tears were streaming down her cheeks.

The past few months had weakened her. She had lost nearly fifteen pounds. Her body wasn't ready for a shock like this one. As she began to try to breathe and take in what was before her, she could not help being nostalgic about the memories that had brought them to this place and moment in time. She slowly opened her eyes and yes, it was real.

Later she gathered her thoughts and reminisced about the stories she had heard that had chartered her life on an unbelievable course. A course that guided her life through a chain of events that led to an unbelievable outcome.

It had all started with Katie 's grandparents, Ed and Belle, her father's parents. Their lives together began on a harsh January morning in the early 1900s. The wedding had taken place before the minister in the country log cabin church with only a handful of family and friends able to attend. Weather conditions were treacherous and by the time the minister arrived, the little wood stove and tall stove pipe were glowing red. The little one-room church was beginning to warm so that the bride could shed her coat for the ceremony.

Outside the cruel blustery wind blew and swirled the snow as it tried to reach the ground. The icy air seemed to creep in around the windows and doors of the old one-room church building. The snow grew deeper and deeper as the pendulum on the big clock hanging on the wall ticked the seconds and minutes away while the pastor married the young couple, pronounced them man and wife and prayed for their future.

Meanwhile the horses pranced and whinnied as they stood hitched to the wagon, waiting to take the newlyweds back to their new home.

Immediately after the ceremony, Ed helped Belle up into the wagon and wrapped the big wool quilt around them both before he raised the reins and smooched to the horses to head out of the drive. Carefully and slowly they proceeded to the small house that would protect them from the elements of this harsh winter. The old farm house had been in the family for years, and there the lives of two young people madly in love began.

The log cabin, built in the 1800s like the old church house, was hard to heat in the Southern Illinois winters. Grandpa had stopped by the house on his way to the wedding to build a fire in the fireplace, so there would be a warm hearth to welcome them home.

Gram had shared the story of her wedding day with Katie on several occasions, as well as the tale of how hot the temperature had risen in late July.

"I told Ed, as he was carrying in an armful of sticks for

the cook stove, 'I'll try to remember next winter when it is cold, just how hot it is today.'"

"You know, Katie, you can always put on more clothes and sit closer to the fire, but you just couldn't get cool, especially when you had to build a fire in the cook stove for coffee first thing in the morning."

There was no running water or electricity, but this had not seemed so disturbing at the time, because these were luxuries. No one they knew was able to afford to be so extravagant.

Neither the heat nor freezing cold temperatures dampened their spirits. They were in love and planning their future, which included a big family.

For so many years Ed and Belle were such poor people; however, they were rich in their love for each other, and their faith in God. In return God had blessed them with five children. There was little Sarrie, a cute little blue-eyed, serious child, Then there was Ben, a dark-haired, brown-eyed stubborn little boy who wanted to do things his way. But when he smiled, he won everyone's heart.

Luke was next, also dark-headed, and he was a people pleaser, sometimes up to a little meanness, but always loved to make the family laugh.

James and Maggie were last, not twins but close in age and best buddies. They had been born as World War 1 was starting. Neither child had a better friend than each other and this seemed to be deeply rooted for both of them. This friendship and bond was carried throughout their lives. As little children they both had light blonde hair and blue eyes, smiled a lot and loved nothing better than running and playing together. Happy children and sometimes a little mischievous.

Ed and Belle had been married nearly thirty years and their children all grown when the man knocked on their door wanting to lease their land for oil. They couldn't believe it, but the oil company actually wanted to drill an oil well on their property.

The couple looked forward to the drilling and anxiously watched when they set up the tall drilling rig. Excitement was in the air.

The drilling of the one oil well brought money in and changed their lives tremendously.

They monitored the drilling of their oil well with great anticipation. Katie heard the story so many times she felt like she had helped drill the well.

At last, after several days of watching the well and waiting anxiously, one evening the geologist who was monitoring the well said, "We are nearing the Benoist formation. It is, as I'm sure you already know, the formation where we are hoping to hit oil. Barring any unforeseen trouble, we should be tapping that pay zone, maybe around midnight."

How thrilling, Ed thought. Within a few more hours he would know if the hole would in fact make an oil well. They were drilling down about a foot every three minutes. He looked up at the western sky and could tell by the angle of the sun that Belle would be putting supper on the table soon.

"If you guys think it will be midnight before you get to the Benoist, I think I'll go have some supper. I want to be here when you find out if there is any oil down that hole. By the way, why do they call that formation the Benoist?" Ed asked.

"Well, there was a family by the name of Benoist and someone drilled an oil well on their ground and found oil in this formation. The way the story goes, they drilled a bunch of wells on their ground. It was here in the Illinois Basin and all the wells had oil in the same formation, so they just named it after the family who had so many wells," the geologist said.

"Wow," Ed said, as he shook his head, "now wouldn't that be something?"

Ed never forgot to put that part in the story every time he told about the drilling of his well. He thought that would really be something to have enough oil to name a formation after your family.

He walked up to the old rundown house where they had raised their family. As he opened the back door, Belle was taking cornbread out of the oven. "Sure smells good in here but sure is hot. Let's eat out in the backyard."

There was a breeze blowing and it was comfortable sitting out under the tree. They could hear the motor on the rig grinding away, as it continued to drill down deeper and deeper.

"You know, Belle, if we hit some oil, I'm going to build you a new house," Ed said.

"I'm looking forward to it, I sure am," Belle said.

Belle had described that evening so many times, Katie could almost see them sitting out under the old maple tree with their hair blowing in the light breeze. There was nothing but the stump left now, but the old tree had shaded many little picnic lunches for Katie and her grandparents when she was a child.

Gram would always start the story by saying, "We was a sit'n in the shade of that tree over there and hav'n a bite to eat when Dad promised me this house, and he kept his word. He was a good man, one of the best God made."

After supper, as the story went, he then moseyed back to the well. Katie had heard numerous times how when Ed got back down to the well, there was excitement in the air. The geologist had yelled over the loud motors, "We are doing pretty good, Ed. Won't be long now till we know something."

Ed was watching every sample with the geologist and after awhile noticed the motor was straining a little harder to drill down through the rock.

"Hum," the geologist said, "We've hit a harder vein of rock, this may slow us down some."

They broke a drill bit and had to replace that. While this was going on, Ed found a place to sit out of the way. He leaned his head over and soon dozed off.

The drilling went from a foot every three minutes to a foot every ten minutes. Then it went to twelve minutes a foot, the motor working a little harder. Finally, they drilled several feet at fifteen minutes a foot. This was taking longer than expected.

When Ed woke up he heard the men talking about seeing a trace of oil in the last sample. Didn't take him long to get to his feet and look for himself. "Do you think that is going to make a well? Is there enough oil there?" Ed rubbed his eyes and tried to get woke up.

"It is too early to tell, but we'll know something before long. The drilling is getting easier again, only five minutes per foot for the last few feet. Hey, look at this sample. We just brought it up, and there is more oil in this test."

By this time it was nearly dawn and the sky in the east was turning a soft glowing orange as Ed looked out across the field. Drilling had taken several more hours than expected to get to the Benoist formation.

The excitement mounted and in about thirty minutes there was quite a bit of oil in each sample that came up. Ed couldn't wait to get home and tell Belle.

There really had been enough oil to make a well, the casing was soon set, and a pumpjack put in place. It wasn't long till Belle and Ed were receiving their monthly oil checks.

They saved their money and soon had enough to start

their long-awaited house. Ed and the boys did most of the work themselves. They had cut several trees from the back woods and hauled them to the sawmill. Every few days they would hitch up the team of horses, take some logs for sawing, and pick up the lumber from the logs that had previously been taken in.

The sawmill was in Woodlawn, not too far from their home. The little town of Woodlawn had been built up around two sawmills. Grandpa was related, down the line, to old man Woods, who had started the sawmill on the south side of the tracks. The community was named after the Woods family and had continued to grow through the years. Main Steet consisted of a feed store, grocery store and post office. Grandpa would take grandma and her eggs to do her tradin' once a week.

The sawmill was powered by a huge steam engine. The huge, very long, wide belt traveled from the steam engine's pulley to the pulley on the mill turning the saw. As the steam built up in the engine, giving more power to the mill, the saw turned faster and faster.

The old stories grandpa and grandma told of earlier days had always intrigued Katie and she never tired of hearing them. The story of how Woodlawn had started and how grandpa had taken trees from his woods to have them sawed at the sawmill for their home was history, and Katie savored every word.

As the oil well pumped and brought the oil to the surface, it made a tremendous noise each time the pumpjack went up and down, clanging and banging, that some of the neighbors asked, "Ed, doesn't that noise bother you?"

Ed would always answer, with a chuckle, "No, it doesn't bother me near as much as when it stops!"

Chapter 2

Two of Ed and Belle's sons, Luke and James, were called to serve their country during World War II. They went proudly to protect and defend the USA. While Luke was in Germany, nearly freezing to death during the frigid winters, seeing more blood and death than he had ever imagined; James was in a war zone himself in the Philippines, and working with Dr. Kofelt in the medics unit. The injuries James witnessed were something that would stay with him for his lifetime. He became quite skillful at stitching human flesh to repair gapping wounds. He learned to set bones, and bandage severe injuries. Dr. Kofelt was impressed with his talent, and at the end of the war asked him to come to his hometown and work with him in his office.

The older brother was married and had children by the time World War II was underway, so he stayed home and worked.

When the boys left for the war the house and barn were well underway, only needing a few finishing touches here and there.

Ed and Belle prayed each day for the safe return of both boys. Belle wrote to each boy several times a week without fail, trying to give each one encouragement and some news of the community, of their friends, and brighten their day as they received and read a letter from home.

She always included a paragraph telling them of the progress of the new house. She was so proud of the flower beds Ed had made; she always noted something about them in the letters too. The colors of the flowers seemed to sparkle in the sun as she stood on the front porch and looked out over the yard and flower beds.

The boys would always ask if the oil well was still clanging and banging in their return letters. They were always glad to hear from home, but as with so many of the soldiers, a few tears always seemed to escape and trickle down their cheeks as they read the letters.

Each soldier became involved with their buddies' families and their lives at home. So when James would get a letter, everyone wanted to know if the oil well was still clanging. A couple of the nurses were always interested in the flower beds.

In the mid '40s they completed their new home. They were able to move from a farm house with no comforts at all to a home with running water and an inside bathroom.

Lighting both the living and dining rooms were prominent chandeliers that hung from the center of each room. When the droplet prisms that encircled the chandeliers caught the sun's rays they projected a beautiful and sparkling display. Belle kept them so clean that the sun would glisten across the rooms, causing colors to dance on the walls.

Moving to the new home was such a very dramatic change in their lifestyle. Only on rare occasions were they allowed to use the inside toilet. Belle still wanted everyone to use the old outhouse. She was famous for saying, "Flushing that toilet just wastes too much water."

Katie could well remember the toilet incidents. Gram would make her go outside to the toilet in the humid, sultry 100-degree temperatures, and more than once she had opened the door to discover a snake laying on the cool concrete floor of the WPA toilet.

The fireplace in the living room was one of Ed's favorite segments of the house. He had chosen slick yellow-glazed brick for the front of the fireplace. They were very unique, as well as the inglenook he had built to make the fireplace truly the main attraction in the living room.

Katie had only seen one other fireplace with yellow brick and that was on a television program, "Restoring America." The yellow brick, together with the striking walnut beam that Ed had hewn from a huge walnut tree for the mantel, made for an outstanding fireplace. The walnut tree had stood for years, but had to be cut to make room for the new house.

Another one of Belle's quirks was keeping the fireplace clean, so an actual fire was never built in the fireplace while Ed was alive. Nonetheless, the couple had enjoyed the electric logs, which for that day and age looked very authentic. Ed had to be content with the look and not the comfort of the warm fire.

The house and barn both stood new, beautiful, inviting and complete as the family servicemen returned from World War II. Katie could visualize that day in her mind. Yet another one of the stories told and retold through the years was of her dad coming in to Puget Sound, Washington.

As the ship came in to Puget Sound, Washington, the men, seeing the soil of the United States of America for the first time in three years, joined in a rousing "USA, USA, USA" cheer. It was a wonderful sight, absolutely breathtaking, bringing tears to nearly every eye on the ship.

The passenger trains were loaded beyond capacity with soldiers anxious to return to their homes and families. Trains were headed in all directions taking the men to their home states. There had been such a crowd of men, of course, that there were layovers sometimes, and the trip home took several days. James had no way of knowing when he would be home and no way of letting his folks know he was on his way.

The last leg of the trip was on a Greyhound bus and as it was going east on Highway 15, across Southern Illinois, it was bringing the youngest brother, James, closer to home and family. He went up to the driver and said, "I live right up there, about a quarter of a mile. Could I just get off and walk home, rather than riding into the next town?"

"Sure, soldier! You just tell me where to stop."

"The next road there at the top of that hill, just pull over off there on the right-hand side of the highway. I'd sure appreciate it. Thank you."

The bus pulled up for a stop and when the driver opened the door, he said, "Thank YOU, soldier."

All the people on the bus simultaneously yelled "Good luck," or "Thanks, soldier."

He waved and started walking home as the bus pulled away. Entering the driveway, James could see how much work his folks had done toward finishing up the house. The flower beds created by his dad were just as beautiful as his mom had written. It was awesome to be home. He had never felt so relieved. It was almost breathtaking to be standing once again in his own front yard, and to be looking at the house he had helped build. At times when the mortar fire had been so close, he felt that he would never see this place or his parents again. He took a moment to stop, look up to the heavens, and thank his Heavenly Father for his safe return.

When he walked in the house, his mother was bent over the oven, removing an apple pie. She was so excited, quickly setting the apple pie on the table, she screamed and cried, and above all didn't want to stop hugging him. She finally said, "Your dad is out back toward the oil well. He will be thrilled to see you. Come on, come on, let's go see him."

After being away so long, the back yard looked inviting and familiar. They were almost trotting as they started down the lane. James was amazed at how fast him mom could travel. As he approached, he saw his dad and waved. He heard his dad exclaim, "THERE'S MY BOY! THERE'S MY BOY!" Running to each other, they were soon in each other's arms and it had never felt so good to have his dad's arms around him.

Katie felt as though she had been on the bus, waved to that soldier coming home, and walked down the road with her dad when he laid eyes on the beautiful finished house for the first time.

But that was long ago, and times kept changing.

Chapter 3

Ed had been a wonderful husband and father to the couple's five children. Grown now and with families of their own, the children and grandchildren loved to come and visit.

Ed had loved to sit in the big swing on the front porch looking out over the fields. He would think about how God had blessed him through the years, by giving him Belle and his wonderful family.

Ed's oil well had not been as prosperous as his brothers' wells. Soon after the house was finished, the oil well had stopped pumping, although many of the other oil wells in the area had continued to pump for years and years.

He had always wondered why his brothers' wells had kept on pumping year after year and continued to bring in a sizable check. His well, although located on a neighboring forty-acre tract, had gone dry after pumping for little more than a couple years. He had always wondered if it was God's will, or had the oil company done something to the well when they fracked it. They had fracked it a couple times and it had never pumped quite the same after that. Fracking an oil well was a process by which they forced sand down the well to bring up more oil. Ed always thought that maybe it brought up more water instead of oil. He had heard stories about how fracking wells sometimes ruined the well. Finally, the well was plugged. Obviously, that brought an abrupt stop to the oil checks.

The oil well, although it didn't pump for many years like some of his brothers' wells, had given Ed and Belle enough money to build their new house. It had also given him and his family extra money, which had bought Belle a fur coat similar to her sister-in-laws'. All three of the sister-in-laws had purchased a fur coat with their oil money. Katie and one of her cousins had dressed as gorillas for Halloween in later years, wearing their grandmother's fur coats.

Ed and Belle had also purchased a Ford car. Katie could remember that old car. They had it even after she was born. It was the prettiest blue, and Grandma and Grandpa were so proud of it. They never let it get dirty. Sometimes when she was a little girl, Katie would accompany Grandma and Grandpa to Woodlawn for groceries. Grandpa would always buy her a Hershey candy bar, and to this day, the smell of a Hershey bar gave her a warm feeling inside, remembering Grandpa and how he'd given her a nickel to pay for the Hershey bar.

Ed and Belle were happy that they had been able to contribute to the neighborhood church. They had been able to help pay for the roof job the church so desperately needed with some of their oil money.

Had it not been for the oil well, they would not have had these luxuries. They were very thankful to God for all these good fortunes.

Growing up about a quarter of a mile down the road, Katie was in and out of Grandma and Grandpa's house at least once a day nearly all her childhood. The old house carried more meaning for her than it did for the rest of the family, because she had spent so much time there as a child.

Grandma had the prettiest green carnival glass dishes, and on special occasions she would set the table with the festive dinnerware. Pretty dishes were special to Grandma, and she loved making her table look beautiful and festive when she had company. Katie had always loved it when more of the family came for dinner. Not only was the table pretty, the food was delicious. Grandma had been a wonderful cook.

Easter was Katie's favorite. Grandma made a two-layer cake for Easter that was so light and fluffy it would melt in your mouth. Every year it was the same, white frosting, rabbits made out of marshmallows all around the sides of the cake, and coconut colored green for grass, with jelly beans on top.

Several oil wells were drilled in the neighborhood while Katie was growing up, and she was often allowed to go with her grandpa or dad to the drilling site and check on how they were doing.

Most of the pumpers knew Katie. She was always outside playing or riding her bicycle during the warm months. They always waved and sometimes brought her ice cream from the country store in Woodlawn.

In the mid '50s Ed had a massive heart attack and died within a week. Belle was devastated. She had this big beautiful home but was unable to mow the grass or fix anything that went wrong, big or small. One of her sons, Luke, offered to buy the place. He told her she could live there, rent free, until her death. She lived twelve very lonely years in her charming home. She prayed each day that the good Lord would take her home so that she might once again be with Ed, or Dad, as she had always called him.

Chapter 4

In driving by, one would never know what a beautiful home this big old farmhouse had once been. Years ago the beautiful white two-story home with the handmade banister around the porch had looked as if you just needed to sit down, prop your feet up, and have a glass of lemonade. The house now looked as though the lemonade had soured.

The paint was peeling, the porch swing chain was broken and one end of the swing was dangling down. The windows were so dirty you couldn't see in, or out. When she was younger, Belle had always kept them so clean they sparkled. Belle could have done a commercial for the window cleaner, and that window cleaner was always vinegar and water. She swore that was the best thing in the world for cleaning windows.

Cobwebs were hanging in the corners of the porch, looking like someone had hung Halloween decorations and failed to take them down. They were laden with dirt and dust raised by cars and oil field trucks passing on the road.

Grandpa had always painted the huge barn white, never red as most barns, but it looked forgotten and forlorn now. The weeds were so high you could not see some of the windows, and the ones still visible were broken. Some of the doors were hanging askew and some had fallen to the ground.

The house and barn had deteriorated with age. Slats on the porch had rotted, and on the inside the walls had cracked and needed fixing. It desperately needed a new roof and the yard and grounds needed cleaned up.

Since Katie's graduation from high school she had been working at one of the local oil companies in town, saving every penny, so that when the opportunity presented itself, she would be prepared to move out on her own.

After Belle's death, Katie asked her uncle if she could rent the place, hoping that someday in the not-too-distant future she would be able to purchase the whole forty acres. Luke had always been very fond of his brother's daughter and knew she would love the old home. Katie's dad was a great carpenter, and Luke knew the place would be fixed up. He realized it would be to his advantage to let Katie live there for a modest rent charge.

Luke agreed to pay for some minor repairs and paint, along with a new furnace and roof.

Katie and her father started work immediately on the house and yard. Several weeks of general cleanup and a lot of hard work went into the preparation for Katie's move. Every room had to be painted, the new furnace installed, and caulking around the windows replaced, just to mention a few things.

Finally, with great anticipation, moving day arrived. Katie was elated. There was a lot left to do, but she couldn't wait any longer to move in. She was so excited, she was going to be independent and living on her own, even if it was just down the road from her parents.

It was amazing what a coat of paint here and there

could do. Elbow grease and several batches of Belle's old recipe for window cleaner were used to bring back the luster and sparkle of the window panes. Along with brightly colored petunias and marigolds planted in the old flower beds that Ed had created, each new improvement enhanced the house, giving it new life.

Katie dreamed of raising her family in this wonderful old home. There was so much room and the house just needed a family. She loved the flowing staircase and the kitchen cabinets that her grandpa had built.

In the main floor bedroom, a built-in dresser sat under the staircase, and an archway above it provided a place for a beautifully framed mirror. Katie wished she had the mirror that gram had hung there, but it had been sold as soon as gram had died, along with many other treasures.

The upstairs rooms were used for storage after the children had grown and left home. Katie hoped to one day fall in love, marry, and possibly turn one of those rooms into a nursery, when the time came.

She wanted to start work on the barn, and hoped to maybe someday purchase a horse or two. Katie could still remember all the hours she and her grandpa had spent out at the barn and in the pasture riding the old family horse, Jake. He was just the perfect horse and ever so gentle with her as a little girl. She had always promised herself that someday she would have a horse like that for her children.

There was a community junior college not far from town. The oil company offered to compensate any employee who would further their education, taking courses that would be beneficial to their position within the firm. Accounting and computer courses filled her schedule the first year. The second year her boss suggested she include a geology course. He felt that knowledge would be beneficial for advancement.

Sandwiched between her job, taking classes at the junior college, and working on her grandparents' house, she did not have a lot of extra time. Yard cleanup and mowing had occupied a lot of Katie's time during the summer months. Now, with winter settling in, outside work would be halted and improvements delayed until spring, possibly giving her a break. Perhaps she would be able to attend some of the youth activities at her church. There never seemed to be enough time for socializing with so much work to be done.

Chapter 5

Nick, the young man who sat behind her in the geology class, could not keep from wondering why a girl was interested in geology. After all, a geologist was definitely a man's job. At least, that was what Nick thought. It wouldn't be a job a woman would be interested in.

He noticed how beautiful she was with that coal black hair hanging down her back in loose curls. He would always associate that class with those lovely locks of hair.

Nick had wanted to ask her out, but she never seemed to show interest in him at all. Other than a casual hello if he beat her to class, there was not much communication between them. She would speak when she came in to sit down if he was already there, and he made it a point to be there when she arrived. He would do anything to have her smile at him and say a quick hello.

She always left right after class, never hanging around to visit or socialize with anyone. This led Nick to assume she had a boyfriend and wasn't interested in meeting someone new. He, on the other hand, had many friends, and one of them always had something to tell him or a new joke to pass along after class. While Nick had lots of friends and went out often, there was no one special. He thought Katie was beautiful, and wanted to get to know her.

One particular January evening after geology class as he was going out to his pickup, he noticed Katie across the parking lot. He thought it was strange she had not left the lot, as class had been over for nearly thirty minutes. Nick saw that the predicted snowfall had arrived, and had accumulated close to two inches. As he got closer, he observed that she had a flat tire. He would have changed all four tires, rotated them and changed them all back if she had asked him to. Katie was so preoccupied with how to get the tire changed and getting home before the snow got any deeper, that she was unaware of Nick crossing the parking lot, heading in her direction, until he called out, "You know, I could probably change that tire for you if you would go for a cup of coffee with me afterwards."

Startled, Katie looked up and for the first time noticed how strikingly handsome Nick was, and his smile melted her heart. The streetlights on the parking lot were bright and the blue in his eyes sparkled in the light.

Knowing Nick from class she felt safe and knew he meant no harm. She said, "I'd be happy to buy you the cup of coffee, but with this snow coming down, I really need to get home. But, I tell you what, if you will change my tire, I will buy you supper Saturday night, any place you want to eat."

Nick grinned, as his beautiful blue eyes twinkled. "Okay, I'll be glad to change the tire, but I will buy your supper."

Katie smiled. "We will settle that when the check comes on Saturday night. Right now, I just need my tire changed."

"Get in the car where it is warmer, you don't have to stay out here with me," Nick said.

She was determined to stand out in the cold in case she could help him in some way. He felt comfortable having her close by, and enjoyed the light conversation they had while he changed the tire. Nick would have loved to take longer with the tire, but he hated seeing her shivering in the cold, and the snowfall was increasing. He finished his good samaritan deed in record time.

Wiping his hands on the towel Katie handed him from the trunk of her car, he winked and said, "I really need your phone number so I can call you to finalize plans for this dinner you promised to buy me."

"That is a good idea, and I WILL be buying your dinner on Saturday, because I really do appreciate your help."

"Could you write it down for me? I'm afraid I won't be able to remember it, my brain feels frozen. You look frozen, too. You better get in and get on your way home. I'll make sure your car starts before I leave," Nick said.

"Oh, thank you so much Nick. I'm not sure I could have changed it myself, especially in this snow. Dad tried to show me how to do this once, but I guess I should have paid more attention. Thank you again," Katie replied.

As he got in his pickup, he knew he would not be able to stand the wait till Saturday evening. It was only Wednesday and he was looking forward to just being in her company. Katie was a beautiful, intelligent young girl and Nick was sure they would have a good evening. He could already tell that from the short time they had talked while he was changing the tire.

Nick was a good-looking, tall, blond-haired, blue-eyed, rugged looking individual. In high school, he had been on the basketball team, had made good grades, and was popular with the girls. He had dated several, but didn't really get serious with any of them.

Katie lived twenty-five miles from the school and it

was a long drive home. Her hands hurt from gripping the steering wheel and her eyes felt as though she had not blinked since she left the college. The snow was coming down so hard now that she struggled to see the road on the way home and some places were becoming slick and treacherous. She finally reached her house, exhausted and relieved. The wind was picking up and Katie knew from experience that there would be drifts everywhere in the morning.

She made a mental note that one of the first things she was going to renovate in the spring was the garage. The double doors had sagged and did not open easily even when the ground wasn't frozen. With the wind picking up and the snow blowing, using the garage was out of the question. Katie parked the car close to the sidewalk leading to the front door, grabbed her books, and hurried into the house. She was thankful to be home.

Katie had laid everything out for a fire before she left for school, down to the crumpled paper under the twigs. Katie put a match to the papers, and in no time the blaze was catching the twigs, and soon putting out a beautiful glow, and even giving off some heat. She quickly made some hot cocoa, sat down in her favorite chair close to the fire, and tried to relax. She laid her head back and was glad that grandpa had insisted on the fireplace. Although he was never able to enjoy the warmth of the fire, she did, and she planned to for many years to come.

She took a deep breath and at last took a minute to thank God that she had made it safely home and for sending Nick to her rescue.

Concentrating so hard on driving home, she had not really had time to think of Nick. Now that he came to mind, it brought a smile to her face. How had she not noticed that he was so good looking?

"What is wrong with you, Katie?" she said aloud, as she curled up under one of gram's old quilts, with a steaming cup of hot chocolate.

She reminded herself that she did not have time for a love life at this point. However, she found herself looking forward to the Saturday evening get together. Nick had seemed very nice to be with, and she was hoping they would enjoy being together.

Interrupting her little daydream, the phone's sharp ring broke her chain of thought.

"Hello."

"Hello, Katie, is that you?" Nick said.

"Yes, it's me." She knew immediately that the voice belonged to Nick.

"I just had to call and see if you made it home safely," Nick said.

"That was so nice of you. Thank you for calling. Did you have any trouble getting home?"

"No, I didn't, but I had to stop and pull one guy out of the ditch on our road."

"You were quite the good samaritan tonight then, saving me and someone else, too. Are they going to take you out to eat?" Katie was hoping that it wasn't another gal and that he had made another date.

Nick laughed. "No, you are the only one I have a date with. This was an old man."

"Good," Katie said. "Thanks for calling and thank you even more for changing my tire." Katie didn't really want to hang up. It had been so nice of him to call and check on her.

"You may have to help me study sometime to repay the favor," Nick said.

"Oh, I'd be glad to help, we can study together," hoping she didn't sound too over anxious.

"Well, I better let you go, I'll see you Saturday night, I'm looking forward to it."

"So am I. I'll see you then. Good night."

Wanting to see the ten o'clock news to hear the weather to see how much snow they were expecting, she sat there for a while, so nice and warm under the quilt. Gram would have said she was "as snug as a bug in a rug." This made Katie smile, to think of her favorite phrase.

Katie dozed off and missed the weather forecast and the fire was dying down when she opened her eyes. She dragged herself from the comfort of the quilt and closed the glass doors on the fireplace. Katie quickly got ready and was soon snuggled in bed. Contentedly she drifted off to sleep, thinking of Nick and their Saturday evening plans.

Chapter 6

Both the telephone and alarm were ringing at the same time bringing Katie straight up in bed the next morning. Her boss was on the line. "Have you seen all the snow? There is no way you will be able to get to work this morning. Almost everything has closed for the day because of the snow. Just stay inside and take it easy. Hopefully the snow plows will be out and we will see you tomorrow."

After she got herself awake, she went to look out front, and not only had it snowed all night, but it had also blown and drifted the snow. The drift behind her car looked at least waist deep. The wind had died down, but it was still snowing. The flakes were so big it looked as though someone was spilling a bag of cotton balls and they were softly swaying to the ground.

She made a pot of coffee and planned to get the fire going in her grandpa's huge fireplace and then settle down to study. She had a couple assignments that were due shortly and she was going to take advantage of the extra time she had to get them done.

When she finally looked at the clock, she realized she had been working on her studies for about five hours. It was nearly one p.m. The time had flown. There had been virtually no interruptions, and she had accomplished a great deal. She then decided it was time to shower, get dressed and have lunch. She had done enough studying for one day.

The tuna fish sandwich on toast was satisfying, and the ice cream she allowed herself for dessert was a welcome treat. She felt refreshed and eager to start another project.

Katie thought it would be a perfect time to go upstairs and dig through the old trunk that had belonged to her grandma. The trunk had been in the family for years, having been passed down from gram's granny and then Katie had inherited it when gram died.

Gram had been working on a quilt when her health had started failing, and Katie knew there were scraps in the trunk, probably enough to finish that quilt top.

Katie couldn't recall the last time she had seen gram work on her quilts. When Katie was little, she could remember gram sitting in her big wooden rocker, hand sewing the blocks together, while grandpa sat in his chair with one leg thrown over one arm of his big chair, cutting the blocks for grandma. He used her special sewing scissors and a cardboard pattern.

Once she had gotten upstairs and found out how cold it was, she decided to put the quilt blocks in a box and bring them downstairs. She had closed the doors to the upstairs rooms as there was no need heating them. She quickly put some of the scraps in a box, and down the stairs she went. Katie couldn't believe the contrast in temperature.

Sitting in front of the fire, she would go through the treasure box and see what she could accomplish. She knew very well how to hand sew. Katie had spent many hours with gram as a child, and gram insisted she learn to sew.

Grandma always made Katie wear a thimble when she sat down to sew. "My granddaughter is not going to have sore fingers from sewing," gram would say.

Unpacking the quilt scraps was overwhelming for Katie. It brought back more memories. Gram had made a dress for her when she started school from the pink flowered piece. The blue checked piece was from a skirt for one of her birthdays.

Katie remembered gram's everyday dress from the scrap with purple flowers. She had worn it a lot. It seemed as if she could remember grandpa bragging on that dress. That was probably why gram wore it so much. As she picked up each piece, it brought back some faint memory.

There, in a little paper bag, she found the cardboard patterns and the scissors grandpa had used so many years ago. Several blocks, cut in the familiar hexagon shape that went with the few already sewn together, were stuffed in the bag, too. And there, in the bottom of the paper sack was a very small thimble. It wouldn't fit her finger now, but she knew it was the same one she had worn as a child, when she sat near her grandma and struggled to sew the little pieces together to make a doll quilt.

Katie went to her sewing box and got a spool of thread and her favorite thimble. Before getting comfortable, she put some wood on the fire. Soon absorbed in the memories, she carefully sewed each piece together.

When the phone rang, it startled her. She jumped and stuck her finger with the needle. "Ouch!"

When she heard the voice on the other end, she forgot about the finger stabbing and was thrilled that Nick had called.

"How ya making it in the blizzard, are you staying warm?"

"I sure am. I'm snuggled up here by the fireplace, soaking up the heat," she said.

"Here I've been out in the cold working with the cattle and grandpa's horses, and you've been in where it is warm as toast," Nick kidded her.

"Well, I did go upstairs, and it isn't heated up there. I got some of gram's old quilt scraps and brought them downstairs. I'm going to finish her quilt." Katie said.

"Oh, my, you went upstairs! I hope the wind wasn't blowing too hard up there. You didn't get frostbite did you?" he laughed as he asked her.

"No, I didn't, but I did get a couple of those assignments completed and out of the way. If you talk a little nicer to me I might give you some tips to help you out," she snapped back jokingly.

"Hey, I can be as nice as the next guy, and even say please if you would help me. Right now I had better go. Dad and my brother are waiting on me. How does 6:30 sound at the new restaurant they just opened in town? That is if it doesn't snow again."

"Sounds great, I'll see you there."

The radio was reporting more snow coming in, but for right now it had stopped for a while. Katie was looking out over the yard and wondering how many inches had fallen. It was hard to tell exactly, with all the blowing and drifting, but she was sure it would be a record snowfall.

After the phone call, Katie took time to fix herself supper and then went back to sewing on the quilt blocks. Looking back over the day, she had enjoyed the time off work and felt she had used her time wisely. She was proud of herself. She delighted in watching as the quilt block came together, and thought to herself, gram would be proud of me for working on her unfinished quilt top. But the highlight of her day had been talking with Nick.

Katie found herself anxiously awaiting the appointed time to meet Nick. She had only a couple more days to wait, and she was eagerly looking forward to going out with him.

Could she call it a date? Would there be any more dates after Saturday night? Or, would this just be payback for the tire change? She certainly hoped that would not be the case.

Friday morning arrived and the sun came up to light up a sparkling wonderland. The snow was so beautiful. At least a couple more inches had fallen during the night. It was like a dream world the way it had accumulated on the tree branches and porch railings. The wind had died down and the snow that had fallen during the night had just cascaded lightly to the ground. It had accumulated on whatever there was between the sky and the ground. It was a picture out of a magazine framed by the window casing in her living room. The sun made the snow twinkle and sparkle as though God had covered the landscape with marshmallows and sprinkled it with glitter.

The phone rang and once again it was her boss. "Katie, there is no use trying to come in to work today. The town is still nearly at a standstill. I heard that they are bringing in big machinery from neighboring towns that haven't had as much snow, to try to help in clearing the streets. They are going to haul it down to Rend Lake and dump it there.

Katie was in hopes the township workers would be out with the road grader today and clear her road off to the highway. She didn't live too far off the state route, and if they got her road cleared, she felt sure the state highway would be cleared, and she would be able to get to town by Saturday night. She knew her dad would let her borrow his four-wheel-drive truck.

After breakfast she put on her snowsuit and brought

in some more wood for the fireplace. Katie planned on another afternoon of sewing in front of the fire, with some music on in the background. She was looking forward to a repeat of yesterday afternoon. First, she was going to walk down to see her folks. They lived in the same house she grew up in, just down the road.

The snowfall was so exquisite, she just had to get out and inhale some of the fresh air, maybe take a few pictures. After an early lunch and visit with her folks, she returned home. She was coming in the door just as the phone was ringing. She answered it rather breathlessly, and heard Nick's voice on the other end. He was curious as to what she was doing that had rendered her so out of breath. She told him she had been out playing in the snow.

"Can I come pick you up for our date? I don't want to worry about you out on these bad roads, and I know for a fact that you don't have a spare tire," he said.

"You know, you are right, I don't have a spare tire. I'll have to get that fixed sometime soon. Don't worry about me. I'm used to handling this. I've always been out here in the country. Besides, I can borrow Dad's four-wheel-drive pickup," she said.

"Well, if you are certain, but I sure don't want you to get hurt, especially coming to see me. I'm really looking forward to Saturday night. It will be good to see you."

"I'm looking forward to Saturday, too," she admitted.

Katie smiled. Nick had referred to their meeting as a date. She liked that.

Chapter 7

The snow finally stopped and the wind had subsided, so the cleanup crews worked diligently through the night and all day Saturday cleaning the roads.

By Saturday evening people were out all over town. They had been snowbound for several days and everyone needed to restock groceries and toilet paper. Some people just had cabin fever and wanted to get out for the evening.

On the drive to town, Katie noticed that many of the houses that had young children living in them had a big snowman in the front yard. She loved snowmen. She had to smile when she saw one, big or small.

Nick and Katie arrived about the same time at the restaurant, and after a short wait, they were seated at a table for two. They discovered they liked many of the same foods and they enjoyed hearing what each other had been doing during the snowstorm.

"My two nieces and I made the neatest gigantic snowman. He looked like Frosty himself," Nick said.

"That sounds like so much fun. I wish I had a big snowman in my yard."

"I bet my nieces would love to come out and help you

tomorrow after church. But you realize I would have to come too, because they are too small to drive," he said with a grin. "Would that be inviting myself out to your house?"

"Yes, it sort of looks that way, but if you guys help build a snowman, I'll forgive you. What are your nieces' names, and how old are they?" she asked.

"Jodi and Cassie, they are Mark's girls. Mark is my older brother, and his wife is Anna. She would like you, and I think you would like her, too. We will have to get together sometime. But back to those girls, I love them to pieces. They are really good girls, and really cute. I tell Mark all the time they look like their Uncle Nick, good looks, charm and charisma. And really they do look like me, but Mark and I look enough alike to be twins. They are the cutest little blonde-haired blue-eyed girls you have ever seen. Jodi is eight and Cassie is six," Nick said.

"I can't wait to meet them. Will you really come out tomorrow afternoon and build me a snowman?" Katie asked.

"Have you got hot chocolate with marshmallows? Cassie and me, we have to have marshmallows in our hot chocolate,"

"Well of course I have hot chocolate and if you have hot chocolate, you have to have marshmallows. I agree," Katie said.

"Then we'll be there. One fat snowman coming up!"

"I'm almost afraid to ask, will he have good looks, charm and charisma?" Katie laughingly teased.

After supper, they decided it was too early to call it an evening. The theater in town was showing a new release that neither had seen. The movie had high ratings, and they both wanted to see it. They discovered they both liked horses and this one was about a horse trainer; seemed like the perfect movie for them to see on their first date.

On the way home, Katie felt so excited about her evening, and the fact that Nick had held her hand during the show. She could hardly wait till tomorrow to see him again.

Katie went to the early service at church and the preacher had preached a sermon that seemed to be directed at her. He read several scriptures that helped her feelings toward meeting new people and making a good impression. After the sermon, she felt uplifted and ready to meet the day, and the girls.

Refreshments for the snowman crew were top on Katie's priority list. She hurried home and decided she would make some homemade cookies to go with the hot chocolate. The Bible says that God helps those who help themselves; and hot chocolate and cookies are always good helpers, no matter what the age.

Nick arrived with Jodi and Cassie and Katie fell in love with them immediately. Adorable girls, and they had coveralls just like Uncle Nick. Both had Nick's beautiful eyes, they were just too cute. They were ready for a snowman party, and the snow was perfect for sticking together and making a ball.

The girls were anxious to get started. They were excited about building the snowman, and they already had on their snowsuits, so there was no time for a tour of the inside of the house before the snowman creation.

Nick got a snowball started. They rolled and rolled and rolled, and it got so big it took all of them to push it. The problem arose when they started with the second ball. How were they going to get it on top of the first one? Katie thought of an old ladder in the garage, and went in the side door to retrieve it. Nick was a little doubtful, but Katie remembered her dad doing this one time. They all worked together and pushed the second ball up the ladder on top of the first ball.

Next came the head of the snowman. Katie left Nick and the girls making the smaller ball as she went to find the scarf she had thought of earlier. Bright red plaid, she thought that would be perfect. She came out with a BIG, really big, pair of sunglasses, a carrot, and the bright red scarf. She had also located an old straw hat that she thought might work. It was the best she could do. The girls laughed and laughed at the snowman with sunglasses and a straw hat. When the snowman was complete, he looked extraordinary.

"Wait just a minute," Katie said. "I want to get some pictures of Frosty here with the building crew. Girls, stand close with Uncle Nick, please, so I can get a group photo. Great. Now let me take a couple more from this angle.

"Thank you so much everyone. I just love him. I'll be the envy of all the neighbors with my beautiful snowman. Come on in, I have cookies and hot chocolate," Katie said as she led the way to the door.

"Good, my hands are freezing Uncle Nick," Jodi whispered, "and my nose is running."

"Do you have marshmallows to go with the hot chocolate?" Cassie asked.

"Of course I do, and my nose is running too, Jodi, plus my eyes are watering. I'll get us a box of tissues as soon as we get inside," Katie answered.

Everyone was ready for a snack and some hot chocolate and some heat. When they stepped inside the house, the welcoming fireplace mesmerized Nick and the girls with the warm fire glowing behind the glass door.

"Here girls, let me help you get your boots off here at

the door, so we don't get snow on Katie's wood floors," Nick offered.

"Thanks, Uncle Nick," Jodi said as she handed the coveralls to Nick to hang up and threw him a kiss.

"Tanks, Unc," Cassie said as she tossed him her coveralls and headed for the fireplace.

Katie pushed her big ottoman over in front of the fireplace and motioned for the girls. "Come over here and sit and let me wrap this flannel quilt around you."

"Oh, Katie, thank you," Jodi said. "It is so soft and warm" and she pulled it tighter around her.

"Yeah, tanks, Katie. It is pitty, isn't it, Jodi?" Cassie asked.

"Cassie, try to talk like a big girl," Nick corrected.

After a few minutes, Katie disappeared into the kitchen for the snacks. When she turned quickly to grab the milk from the refrigerator, she almost ran into Nick. He was standing there watching her. "What can I do to help?"

Katie appreciated the help and they soon returned to the fireplace area with the cookies and hot chocolate. The girls were delighted.

The sun was setting and Nick and Katie were both a little sad to realize their fun day was ending. Nick said, "I need to get the girls home so they can get to bed early for school tomorrow. We both have to get to work in the morning and then classes in the evening," he said.

Just as they were leaving, Katie's dad and mother were going by on their way home. They stopped to admire the snowman. They both loved him. This, of course, thrilled the girls and Katie delighted in introducing Nick and the girls to her folks.

Her folks went on home and Nick got the girls buckled in the pickup. Katie waved and stepped in the house. Just as she was picking up the hot chocolate cups, there was a knock at the door.

She went to the door and there stood Nick. "Can I come in just a second?" he asked.

"Of course, come in. Did the girls forget something?"

"No, I did." Nick said. "I had to come back and thank you for last night and today. I can't tell you how much I enjoyed both times."

"Oh, me, too."

Nick took a step closer to her, reached down, and took her hand. He then laid his right hand on her shoulder, stooped slightly, and gently kissed her on the forehead.

"Could we see each other again? This has been the best weekend I've had in a long time."

"I was hoping you would feel that way," Katie told him. "I loved every minute of this weekend."

"I really do need to get the girls home, but I just had to come back in and say goodbye." He then put his arm around her and so sweetly kissed her on the lips. "Don't forget to get the tire fixed."

Then he was out the door and on the way to this pickup. She was still standing holding onto the door as they backed out and drove away. It had been such a good weekend, and the last few minutes had been so special.

Katie had always loved the snow, but this was definitely the best snowfall she could ever remember. It all had started with a flat tire.

The next morning Katie looked forward to getting back to work and back to the normal routine of things. She was also anxious for geology class. Usually she dreaded going and she had been looking forward to the end of the school year. However, now she was looking at the geology class under a whole new light.

Chapter 8

Finally, the last of the snow melted. Southern Illinois did not have further snowfall that winter, and little by little, spring was creeping up on them.

Katie and Nick continued to see each other and study together as often as possible. They both felt so comfortable when they were in each other's company, and they always laughed and had a good time.

They spent some of their time together studying and working on school projects. Other times they enjoyed going to the show. When the weather cooperated, they went for long walks. Whatever they chose to do, they always took pleasure from each other's company.

Both were looking forward to May and graduation from the local two-year junior college. Nick was going on to a university and eventually hoped to get his degree in agriculture. Katie was going to stay with her job and continue to live in grandpa's house.

Nick had been researching every university in Illinois and the surrounding states that offered an agriculture program. There were several promising agriculture programs in the quad-state region that interested him. However, after reading about the course that Middle

Tennessee State University had to offer, he was more excited than ever about going on to school.

One evening Nick said, "You know, I'd like to become an agricultural teacher, but I want to be more knowledgeable about farming here at home, too. Years and years ago, the people who stayed home and worked on the farm were the people who did not go on to college. Currently with all the modern technology and all the use of chemicals, plus the record keeping involved, you need a good education in order to run a farming business. It is crucial."

"Oh, I can see that, just from being around here the last few months. Your dad amazes me sometimes. He knows how to figure and mix the chemicals so it will be right according to the soil samples. He really surprises me at times. Hey, tell me more about this Tennessee university you want to go to," Katie encouraged.

"When I heard about the program MTSU has, I was very interested. They not only have an outstanding School of Agribusiness and Agriscience, they offer a Horse Science program that is one of the top in the nation. From what I read about their programs, they have at least five faculty and two staff members devoted totally to the horse program, and they may have to hire more soon. It seems they have an awesome arena, too. It is called the Tennessee Miller Coliseum and seats around 6,000 people. Can you believe 6,000 people coming for something horse related? Some of the top horses in the world are brought here, sometimes for shows, sales, or contests of one kind or another."

"I can't begin to imagine a facility of that magnitude," Katie said.

"When I was younger dad had a few horses that Mark and I rode, but grandpa always had horses and he was good with breaking and working with them. I admired that, and I was always interested in horses. Mark says he wishes now that he had attended MTSU for the dairy program. The students have numerous cattle they care for in the dairy curriculum. They process their own milk, and serve it in the cafeteria. Can you believe they take it through the whole process there at the school? It is quite an impressive operation."

"They do the whole thing there at the college?"

"That is what I read. It is not only a learning opportunity, they actually made it profitable for the school. Now they are in the first years of this horse program and I really want to be a part of it. I want to hear more about it and can't wait to get involved. The person I talked to when I called down there was excited about the future developments in horse science. They sent me quite an impressive packet with loads of information on the program. Dad says we will go down one weekend soon and look around."

"That does sound exciting. I don't blame you for choosing that university. Do you think you would want to do something business-wise with the horses or just for pleasure?" Katie asked.

"Well, I hadn't thought about using horses to help make a living, at least not until I started hearing about this program. Now it is in the back of my mind, I have to admit. I guess we will just have to wait and see how this develops and where it leads. I'm hoping you will go with us when we go down to look around"

"Oh, Nick, I'd love to!"

Chapter 9

Katie was making plans to refurbish the garage and have it ready for the following winter so that her new truck wouldn't have to sit outside. After the winter they had been through, she had purchased a new little pickup truck, four-wheel-drive, of course. When she and her dad had gone shopping for the truck, she had no idea what color she wanted, but the one she liked best was a little blue Ford. She had to laugh; there would be, once again, a blue Ford in grandpa's garage some day soon.

She wanted to discuss working on the garage with her uncle when she went by to pay the rent. Hoping to have it complete before winter, she was anxious to get started on it. As usual, she and her dad would do the work, but she needed to talk to her uncle about paying for the supplies.

When she stopped by to pay the rent the following month, she noticed her uncle looked depressed.

"Sit down, Katie, if you have a few minutes," he said.

"Sure, I need to talk to you, too. I was wondering about fixing up the garage."

"Well Katie, I guess we better tell you what we need to talk to you about first," as he took his chair at the end of the table.

She noticed he never let his eyes meet hers. He couldn't seem to face her. At first he looked at the ceiling, and then rested his forehead in his hand, with his arm braced on the table.

"Katie, ya see--well, Katie, it's this way," he stammered.

"Honey, I got something to tell you," he started again.

He cleared his throat several times and tried to start again but words would not come. She noticed there were tears forming in his eyes. At that point his wife intervened, having no trouble spitting out the words, "You'll have to move, Katie. That's just the way it is! Thirty days from now we expect you to be out of the house."

"But why, why do you want me to move? I've taken good care of it, and I pay my rent. I love that old house, it is home. Why do I have to move?" she was trying to be calm, was nearly crying by this time.

Her aunt very calmly told her, "Well, Katie, my daughter by my first marriage, and her family have decided they would like to move out to the country. That would be a perfect place for them, so we are going to let them move in. You need to move so they can get moved in before the school year starts, so their daughter can start school out there."

Katie had taken it for granted that she would continue living in grandpa's house, gradually fixing it up and eventually purchasing it from her uncle. She was astounded when they mentioned her moving. How could this be? They were actually giving her grandpa's place to someone else. This was more than heart breaking, it was unbelievable.

She had thirty days to live in the extraordinary old house. She was devastated. The thought of moving from grandpa's house had never entered her mind. After all the work she and her dad had done, she couldn't imagine moving away from there, not in her wildest dreams.

Instead of talking about renovations as she had planned, was he actually telling her to move? Could she get up from this chair and walk out to her little truck? She had to; she wasn't going to let them see her cry. Her heart was beating so fast, but she did manage to hold back the tears until she got out of their house.

By the time she reached the corner, just out of sight of her uncle's house, she lost control. She cried so hard she could barely get her breath. She laid her head on the steering wheel and continued to weep uncontrollably, until she heard the impatient honking of the old man behind her. She was so upset. The tears would not stop streaming down her face. However, due to the impatience of the man behind her, she cautiously checked both ways and continued on her way home.

Katie thought of her dad. Once again, a new storm of tears formed. He had helped her so much, and together they had put so much love and work into the house. How would he take the news? She dreaded telling him. Katie could not imagine packing up her things and moving to another house.

As soon as she got home she called Nick. She needed to hear his calming voice. When she heard his voice, she immediately started crying, once again.

"Katie , Katie , are you all right? What has happened? Are you hurt?"

"Oh, no, I just found out I have to move. Nick, I love this old house! It is beautiful and dad and I have worked so hard. I haven't told my folks yet, they will be so disappointed, too. I always thought I would end up buying it. I can't bear the thought of living someplace else. Nick, this is just awful. I know that sounds silly but I love it here." She was crying so hard he had a hard time understanding her, but the one thing he did understand was that she was going to have to move out of her grandparents' old farmhouse.

He tried to comfort her over the phone, but was not very successful.

Telling her folks was not something she was looking forward to. After they both got home from work, she went down to break the news. She could not keep from crying as she repeated what her uncle, with his wife's help, had told her. Katie's parents were both upset and disappointed, thinking of all the love they had put into the house. It felt like someone was ripping their daughter's heart out, and they both sensed a feeling of total helplessness.

Her mother tried to console her by saying, "Katie, you must be thankful for the time you were allowed to live there. You will always carry the memories with you through your life. It is only a house, after all. Nick, your father and I are all healthy and you must be thankful for that. It isn't like you lost a loved one. You have to move forward and pray about this part of your life and turn it over to God. I'm sure he will take care of this in his time and this will be a stepping stone to something better."

The first few days after Katie found out she had to move were devastating. She couldn't concentrate at work and her head felt as though it could explode. The simplest things would remind Katie of the old house and the fact she was going to move, and at that point, there would be more tears.

She only had thirty days, so she knew she had to get busy. Would renting or buying be best? She looked at several houses but the payments would far exceed her income. Some of the rental houses were really run down, and she didn't really want to live in town. The decision of where to move was all-consuming. She was desperate to find something, get moved, and get it over with, so she could start a new chapter of her life.

Finally, a friend of hers told her about a house that someone in her family had for sale. "The old house needs a little work, Katie, but the price might be right. The heirs want to get it sold and the estate settled before the end of the year. They might negotiate on the price."

Katie took down the number to call. When she arranged to go look at the house, she made sure it was a time her dad could go with her to see it. Needs a little work was putting it lightly! "I wonder what the inside looks like," she said to her dad when they pulled in the driveway.

She didn't know if she could handle all the work that would be involved. After all, she had just worked on grandpa's house, she wasn't looking forward to another remodeling job, but her dad encouraged her to buy it and he would help her fix it up.

"Katie, you only have thirty days to find a house and move. If you don't do something soon, you will end up living at our house!"

Katie smiled. She knew her dad was trying to kid with her, but when it came to moving, Katie didn't think anything was funny.

"Dad, it doesn't have running water! No running water means no bathroom! No bathroom, no thank you!"

"Come on Katie. It's reasonably priced and we can make several improvements. The structure seems sturdy. There are two wells here close to the house. Celesta, the woman that brought the key, told me the old man who lived here always had plenty of water. You know how we always ran out of water at home. With two wells, you shouldn't run out of water. You know what an inconvenience that would be."

"Of course he had plenty of water! His arm would play

out before he could pump the wells dry. Are you seriously considering me buying this house? You are just kidding me, aren't you. Dad? Please tell me you are kidding."

"No. Seriously Katie, you'll be money ahead. We will get it fixed up, you'll see. We'll have running water and a bathroom before you move in. Then we will do other repairs and fix ups as you can afford them."

"You really can't be serious, Dad! Are you? Dad, there is a hand pump on the kitchen sink. There is no bathroom, I think I've mentioned that before, and there is no furnace. He used coal and wood to heat with, and I don't think I can do that."

"I know and you won't have to," her dad said.

"I have my doubts, but okay, if you think it's best."

Katie reluctantly made an offer, but the heirs held firm on their price and they kept the oil rights. Soon Katie and the heirs came to an agreement. The heirs were very understanding about her lack of time and allowed them to start working on the house immediately, rather than waiting for the closing and legalities to be final.

The house was in need of a lot of repairs and updates. Her dad was a man of his word and he did get the pipes installed for running water and a bathroom in working order before she moved in. The walls weren't painted, and the new plywood on the floor wasn't covered, but at least she could go to the bathroom and take a bath. She hoped that the rest would come soon.

A number of gallons of paint and endless hours of hard work made it livable. Katie was ready to move by the end of the month. More repairs would come later, she hoped soon. But, right now she would just have to live with it the way it was, maybe not as attractive as she would have liked, but at least it was hers. She would try to think of it as camping out.

"I think we can get you moved in one trip with all our pickups," Nick said. He put his arm around her as they sat in grandpa's old porch swing for one last time. "Don't worry. It will be all right. You'll see, things will work out okay."

"That will be great, my friend Jeanne is coming, too. She'll bring her truck and her daughter, Cheryl, will also help. Do I have to be here?" Katie said.

Nick looked down at her. At least she was trying to joke around, he thought. He smiled at her.

"I'm serious, Nick. Do I have to be here? I wish I could be anywhere else."

Moving day got there too fast for Katie, and even though the sun came up in the east, the same as it did every morning, it was the saddest day of her life. She cried nearly all day.

She would never forget the last time she walked through the house. Her furniture was on the trucks and it was merely the bare walls. Her dad held her hand as they walked from room to room, checking the closets and cabinets for any of Katie's personal belongings.

He stopped in front of the front door, just solemnly facing the door, with one hand on the glass doorknob, and said, "You know, Sweetheart, we will probably never be in this house again, so remember all you can." He then opened the front door, walked out onto the front porch and down the steps, and never turned to look back at anything.

As he got in the truck he said, "That's not all I'll never see again." Katie didn't know what he meant at the time, but felt this was not the time to ask.

About eight years later when she heard that her uncle had died, she realized what her dad had meant. In thinking back, she realized that her dad had never seen his brother again after she moved. Her uncle had died a lonely old man after several years in the nursing home. His brother, Katie's dad, had never visited him one time.

Life would go on, she was sure of that, but her new house was so much smaller than grandpa's house and not nearly as accommodating. She resolved to give this place more eye appeal and make it more comfortable. Determined, she tried to save her money and fix up the house.

As they pulled in the drive of her new house, Katie couldn't help but think, there are no family memories here, and there is no porch with a swing for lemonade breaks. She took a deep breath as she climbed out of Nick's truck, and decided she would make her own memories here. If she ended up living here the rest of her life, she would make sure her grandkids had memories of their own to carry forward. Of course, at this point, she couldn't imagine herself with grandkids, and she couldn't imagine them ever being as attached to this homestead as she had been to her grandparents' home. Still, she had a few years to work on the old dwelling. As she looked around, she thought, someday I'll have a front porch here, too.

Yes, God had blessed her in so many ways. She would make this her new home. She was determined.

Katie and her dad would work on one project for a couple weeks and when they thought they were getting that problem fixed, it would lead to another problem. Soon her dad was busy with other jobs he had and there wasn't much time or money spent on the house.

She wanted to make the house a home and make it more cozy and appealing, not just repair and fix things. However, just keeping up with the monthly bills was about all she could handle, there was never enough for the extras.

Sometimes Katie felt so depressed. She tried to tell herself that God had blessed her with the basics and always gave her enough to take care of the problems. In his own time, he would take care of her. She needed to be more patient. Patience, however, was not one of her best traits.

Chapter 10

Nick was always busy helping his family on the farm. He sometimes asked her to come and ride with him if he had to go to the elevator to pick up seed. Sometimes she would just ride in the air-conditioned cab of the tractor with him, and they would enjoy the companionship.

They were becoming such good friends. Nick was so easy to talk to, and they could talk for hours it seemed, never running out of subjects to discuss. He always had a smile and she loved it when he would joke and kid around with her.

Nick's Dad, Carl, farmed several hundred acres, close to a thousand. Nick had one brother, Mark, who lived close by. Mark raised cattle, along with helping Nick and his dad on the farm. Nick and Carl did most of the grain operation, but Mark was always there when they were the busiest.

Katie found that it was fun to be with Nick, and she loved the outdoors. Nick's dad was a very kind, good-hearted man. As he got to know Katie he began to trust her with the family truck, and often asked her to run errands for parts, fertilizer, seed or whatever was needed at the time. He knew she liked to feel needed, and she always wanted to help, if she could.

She loved being part of the operation. Never having been involved with such a large farming undertaking, she had no idea what a complex project planting nearly one thousand acres of corn and beans could be.

It took several dedicated people to keep the machinery in good working order and to have all parts and supplies there when they were needed. She proved to be a great asset to the planting season.

Finally, the crops were in and they could all take a few weeks to relax and enjoy the summer before it was time to start getting the combines ready for harvest. Katie loved being with Nick's family, and they all felt as if she fit in so well they already counted her as part of the family.

Nick and Katie had a busy summer and enjoyed every minute of it. They seemed to have plans every weekend. There was never a dull moment. One weekend they took Mark's girls to the zoo in St. Louis and had so much fun. When they went by the Gateway Arch, the girls thought that would be neat to go up in it, so a few weeks later they all went up in the arch. Nick loved his nieces and they adored their uncle, and had already fallen in love with Katie.

Several times the whole family took the pontoon and went to Rend Lake for the day. What a wonderful time that was for everyone.

Nick and Katie had gone with Mark and Anna to one of the community stage plays a couple of times. The plays, put on by local people, were always outstanding. The entire family enjoyed these evenings. Carl and Sue, of course, delighted with the job of babysitting the girls, and found numerous ways to spoil them.

The evenings were becoming longer. Dark seemed to

be creeping in earlier each evening. Nick commented late one afternoon, "Where did the summer go? I don't think I have ever enjoyed summer so much, but it flew by. It could be because I spent most of my spare time with you."

"I agree with you, summer seems to be slipping away before I'm ready for it to end. You will be leaving for school shortly and I will miss you more than I can tell you. I'm already dreading the long winter evenings without you."

"I'll be home every weekend," Nick said.

Katie had really enjoyed being with Nick's family so much. They had also spent several Sunday afternoons with her folks and Nick felt very comfortable with her family.

"I won't be that far away. I'll miss you too, Katie, more than I want to admit."

Nick had left the small country church that he had attended all his life and had started going with Katie to the Christian church in town. The decision to make the change was a difficult one for Nick. There had been a lot to consider in leaving the country church he had always attended. Family attended that church, there were memories and traditions that were hard to break away from, but the church in town had more to offer someone his age. Most of the people his age that had attended the country church with him as a child had already moved away or were at college.

One Sunday after church, Nick told Katie, "You know, I do miss some of my friends from church. I've known some of those people since I was a small child."

He went on to list some of the life-long members of the church. "There was Vera Jane, she was my first Sunday school teacher, and cared for me in the nursery from the first Sunday I went to church. Then, of course, Mary Margaret, who always had something fun to say to me and gave me an encouraging pat on the back. Her husband, A.

E., always had a smile and a cheery good morning. Mary Ruth and Carroll Ray had helped with the youth group for years."

Katie asked Nick, "Does everyone in your old church have two names?"

"Well, no, not really. It's not like it was a requirement," Nick said. "It seemed as though a lot of people did go by two names. In fact, there were more. My Aunt Mary Alice used to go there, and Peggy Sue the list goes on... and on... One time a new preacher came and he could not believe it. He said it's hard enough to learn one name for everyone, now you expect me to learn two, and with the right combination. We all laughed at him, but he soon caught on.

"Of course, my friends, Lloyd and Ada, they always sat in the same pew every Sunday. They did so much for that little church, as did several others. Lloyd would always pat his foot to the music. Too bad he never heard Drew and the boys in the band at your church. That's just a few of the regulars that were good to me when I was growing up. There were certainly others," Nick explained to Katie .

"I'll miss all those people and memories, but there is just something about your church that draws me into their fold. I would like to get involved with the choir particularly. I have to give up a few things in order to change churches, but the future holds many good things for me, too. It is sort of like you having to move. You give up some things, but I know there are good things in your future, too. Maybe an extremely good-looking guy named Nick, for instance." He smiled and cocked his head, trying to look distinguished.

"It feels like you are truly worshiping the Lord at your church. It is just a feeling that once you go and hear the music and the wonderful message the minister brings each week, you are hooked. I don't want to attend anywhere else. It was hard leaving the people I had attended church with all my life, but I feel good about the change, both during worship and after we leave church. There are so many people our age."

Nick fit in and really enjoyed going with Katie to the activities they had for people their age. He also enjoyed the gospel concerts the church held. Much to Katie's surprise, she learned that he had a beautiful voice himself. He told her that someday he wanted to sing in a group.

He had gone with her to church for several weeks now. She knew that although he had attended the small church with his folks, he had never joined or been baptized. She had prayed for Nick, hoping that he would sometime soon give his life for the Lord.

The last Sunday before he left for college, he invited his parents to the service, too. When they all walked in together, Katie was totally surprised and thrilled. The biggest surprise of all came close to the end of the service, when the minister asked if anyone would like to come forward. Nick stepped out in the aisle, gave her a big smile, and then proceeded down toward the minister.

Katie looked over at Nick's family and could tell that they were as surprised as she was at that moment. Katie could also tell that Nick's folks were both so proud of their son that they were about to burst. The tears streamed down all three of their faces. They could barely contain themselves when the preacher baptized Nick.

Katie had been praying for Nick for quite some time, but hadn't realized that his mother, too, had been praying the same prayer.

After church, Nick's dad took them all out for dinner as a celebration. He said, "I guess the Lord knew when you had Katie and your mother both praying for you, you may as well give in and be baptized."

They laughed, talked, and had a wonderful meal and afternoon that followed.

Nick's dad would soon start the harvest and would miss Nick more than words could express, and his mother was feeling disheartened as well. She couldn't imagine their home without Nick and his big smile. She was immensely proud of her son and the accomplishments he had made, and for going on to further his education, but her motherly instincts were coming through. She knew she would miss him terribly.

Katie was so sad. She had gotten so used to having Nick around, she didn't know what she would do without him close by. They had seen each other several times a week, every week since the spring planting season. Katie knew she would miss him when he left for school.

They were all three happy and excited about him being baptized and starting college in Tennessee, but they knew that at the end of the afternoon he was leaving for school. Katie and his folks had gone down and helped him move in his dorm room earlier in the week. All he had to do today was drive to the dorms. Tomorrow would bring his first day of school, and the beginning of his life away from home.

Katie wondered to herself at how you could feel so excited for someone and sad at the same time. After all, she told herself, he was only going to be gone for a week. Some families were facing sending their loved ones overseas for a year or more. She should be thankful.

As the afternoon slipped by and the hour of Nick's departure was fast approaching, he said, "Katie and I are going for a walk down the lane through the woods."

Nick took Katie's hand as they walked down the lane to the little creek. There, Katie sat on the enormous rocks that lined the side of the creek bed. As Nick paced back and forth, he told Katie, "My grandpa used to tell Mark and I stories of how the Indians had hidden in these rocks and made their arrows out of some of these smaller pieces of flint. He has some really neat arrowheads that he found around here when he was a little boy.

Nick and Katie had gone on walks several times, but never to this exact spot. "Nick, it is truly beautiful here, and the sound of the water trickling over the rocks sounds delightful. I love it back here. It's so shady and cool here," she told Nick as she watched him pacing back and forth.

Katie could tell this place meant a lot to Nick, and she wondered in the back of her mind as to why he had never brought her here before

Just as this thought crossed her mind, Nick took her hand in his and said, "This is one of my very favorite places on the whole farm. I want to explain to you why I have never brought you here. My grandpa always brought my brother and I here when he was in charge of us. He not only told us of stories of Indians being here, he would let us wade in the pools of water. It is pretty shallow now, but sometimes in the spring it gets a little deeper. Mark and I had a lot of fun back here with grandpa.

"There is one place down the creek, sort of back in under some of the sandstone rocks, protected from the weather, where Grandpa showed us one time when the creek was up high. We went by rowboat down the creek a little ways, and there are still some petroglyphs showing. It was awesome. Grandpa had our life jackets on, but when Mom found out that we had been on the creek and the water was that high and running that fast, she wasn't at all happy.

"You can't get there by foot. Grandpa said his grandpa took him down there when he was a boy, and dad confessed later that his grandpa took him down there by boat one time when he was a boy too. Dad said his folks, my grandpa and grandma, weren't too happy either, because even though grandpa knew how dangerous it was, he took us anyway.

"I remember how he cautioned us a hundred times to sit still and not tip the boat, but also telling us that he wanted us to see the writings the Indians had left.

"He told us how his family how come back here for picnics when he was a boy. This place always held a special place in his heart. He told me of one other very special thing that happened here on these rocks."

Katie was captivated and listened intently as Nick proceeded to tell her what his grandpa had told him, of all the happenings in this lovely setting.

"A year ago today my grandpa and I were walking along that field over there and he wanted to walk back up here. We did, and as Grandpa sat on this rock he told me that he had been back here exactly fifty-five years ago to the day of when he and I were here. I was quick to ask him how he remembered where he was fifty-five years ago. He proceeded to tell me that he and my grandma had walked back here and he had asked her to marry him. They were right here where we are sitting, and they were married one year to the day after he proposed to her.

"Katie, I have to tell you that this morning wasn't the last of your surprises for the day. I wanted to keep this place sort of a secret for a while so that when I did bring you here, it would be a very special place for both of us for years to come."

As Nick lowered himself down on one knee on the sandstone rock beside her, he pulled a little white box out of his pocket. "Katie," Nick said, " I would like to ask you to marry me. I wouldn't ask before I was saved, but I do know that I love you more than anything and there will never be anyone else for me. Now that I have been baptized, I want to ask you to spend the rest of your life with me."

When he opened the small ring box, she gasped in surprise. Taking her hand in his, he asked her, "Katie, will you accept this ring as a token of my love and wear it to show everyone you are mine? I know this ring is not the biggest diamond you have ever seen, but I hope that we can work together and someday we will have enough money so I can buy you a much bigger and better ring. I love you very much and I would like you to be my wife."

Nick was so sweet and she loved him so much. To bring her back here to such a special place, to ask her to marry him in the same place his grandpa had asked his grandma. She was already in tears before he had even leaned over to give her a kiss.

Katie would always remember that kiss. It was so breathtakingly romantic. She was tingling from head to toe. When he released her, she felt wobbly, sitting up so high on the rock. She took a deep breath.

Nick put his arm back around her, "Are you all right?"

"Yes, I'm more than all right. It was just that kiss!"

"Oh, well, if there was something wrong with it, maybe I should try again. I want it to be just right." Before she knew it, he was kissing her again, and she loved it. How long they sat there in each other's arms is anyone's guess.

Finally, she said, "Nick, you can't begin to know how much I love you, and my answer is yes! I will always love you, too."

Katie was so surprised she could barely speak. He chose the picture-perfect place to propose and the ideal ring. She said, "Nick, I knew I loved you, but after today I have learned all the more what a kind and loving heart you have. I love you even more."

"More than what? ice cream? brownies? a new sports car? that old house of your grandpa's?"

"Yes, Nick, more than all of those and a million other things you could name. I love you more than I thought possible," She threw her arms around his neck and he lifted her off the rocks.

They had to leave the lovely spot for now, but Katie knew they would be back here several times in their lives.

Nick commented, as they walked back to the house, "I can't wait to tell my grandma and grandpa that you said yes. I told them yesterday what I was going to do, but they were the only ones I told. They both told me you would say yes; and they are thrilled with my choice of girls. By the way Katie, did I tell you how much I love you?"

"I think you did mention that, and I sort of like you, too." Katie laughed.

She could not wait to get back to the house to show Nick's folks the ring and to tell them of the big decision. She was in hopes they would be as thrilled as she was with the new development.

As they walked back up to the house, they could see Nick's grandparents were pulling in the drive. Nick had to laugh. "Look, there is grandpa and grandma pulling in the driveway. They must have been worried that you would say no. They couldn't wait any longer to hear the news."

When they walked in the door his folks and grandparents were sitting in the kitchen. Nick's dad said, "You two both look like you are ready to burst. What's up?"

Grandpa had a big grin on his face, just waiting to hear the official news. Nick said, "Well, I asked her to marry me, but she said no, not a chance."

"I didn't either! I said yes! And now you are stuck with

me until death do us part." She laughed and shook her head at him as she slowly took her hand out of her pocket and held it over for them all to see. There was yet again more excitement and tears. Nick's parents were thrilled that he had made this decision. Everyone was asking questions at once. Did you pick out the ring yourself? When is the wedding? Where are you going to live?

Of course, grandpa and grandma were more than pleased, both about Nick's choice in girls and about the place Nick had chosen to purpose. "I told you boy! I told you she would say yes," Grandpa said as he gave Katie a big bear hug, lifting her completely off the floor.

Nick's dad looked at Nick, then looked at the clock. "Well, son, you have given your mother, Katie, and me quite a day to remember. I don't believe any of us will forget the day you left for college. Do you have any more surprises for us before you leave?"

Everyone laughed and looked at Nick. "That is pretty well the end of my surprises for the day."

Nick knew it was time to leave for his drive to school. He also knew this was starting a new chapter of his life.

Both Katie and Nick said good bye to his family and walked out to Nick's car. Katie told Nick she was going straight to her folks' house to tell them all the exciting news.

"I'll be home Friday night, Katie, and I promise I won't even look at the other girls at school," he said as he hugged her close. Then he got in his car and prepared to leave for school.

Katie told Nick that she was going to start saving her money for the home they would eventually have together.

They pulled out of the driveway, each going their separate ways. Both were ecstatic.

Chapter 11

Katie could not wait to tell her folks of her engagement, so she drove straight to their house. They were as excited as Nick's folks had been. Nick was a God-fearing young man, and they were proud that he had been baptized that morning, and soon would be a part of their family. Nick's whole family had impressed them and the fact that their daughter had chosen a good Christian young man made them proud.

Katie and her mother talked briefly about the kind of wedding she wanted. Her dad kissed her on the cheek and said, "I love you, sweetheart and I'm proud of you. I want you to have the wedding of your dreams. Take your mom shopping and you find the perfect dress for your wedding."

As Katie left her parents' home and drove to her little house, she had to pass the big old farmhouse that had belonged to her grandparents. It made her sad to see it. Although she had just moved from it a few months ago, it already showed signs of neglect. Such a waste, after all the work she and her dad had done on the house, but she told herself, "This is not my worry anymore. Just let it go!"

That was easier said than done. There was junk on the

front porch and trash had blown in the front yard. The grass needed mowing and the shrubs lacked attention. Her uncle had made the decision to give the place to someone else. She had once thought she would always live and raise her family there, but this was not to be. Sometimes things did not turn out as you expected. She looked down at her ring and said aloud, "I will be happy anywhere, as long as I'm with Nick."

On the drive home, Katie remembered the quilt pieces she had brought down from the attic last winter. The quilt was the "Grandmother's Flower Garden" pattern that her own grandma had started piecing many years ago. She was determined to finish it in memory of grandma. "Wouldn't it be something if I finished it in time for my wedding," she said aloud. "That would really be a tribute to grandma."

Throughout the busy summer, time had not given in to working on the quilt. She had spent every minute she could with Nick. When she got home, she got the quilt out of the closet and placed it in a basket on the couch. Knowing if she saw it she would pick it up more frequently, and work on it. She promised herself she would do some on it every day while Nick was at college.

It was getting late now and there had been so much excitement today. Katie knew she needed to get to bed so she would be able to get up and go to work in the morning.

Katie was exhausted, but when she got to bed, she couldn't go to sleep for quite awhile, just thinking about the wonderful day and all the things that had happened. Before she finally closed her eyes to drift off to sleep, she thanked God for all the wonderful blessings that were going on in her life. She also thanked God for putting Nick in her life and asked that he watch over and keep him safe in his travels back and forth to school.

Chapter 12

The ring was on her finger. It hadn't been a dream. That was the first thing Katie checked when she awoke on Monday morning.

She drove to work that morning with a big smile on her face, planning to wait for someone to notice her engagement ring and comment on it before telling anyone. However, as soon as she walked in the door of the office she was so excited she held out her hand for everyone to see. They were all so excited for her and Nick, and wished them the very best in the future.

Everyone listened intently to the story of how Nick had proposed to her in such a special place. The very idea that he had thought to pick the exact same location that his grandfather had proposed to his grandmother was so romantic. The women she worked with all told her what a lucky girl she was, not many men would have thought of doing all he had done.

After work and having had a quick bite of supper, Katie was eager to resume work on the quilt, hoping that it would be completely finished before the wedding. She hurried through the normal chores around the house as quickly as possible so she could spend the rest of the evening stitching on the quilt.

By bedtime she had nearly completed another flower garden block. She had many stitches to make before the quilt would be complete, but she was excited about working on it. In order to make the quilt large enough for the bed, it was going to take several blocks set together. This would involve many nights and thousands of stitches. There would be a lot of time for her to work on it while Nick was finishing his education.

The following day was a carbon copy of Monday, home from work and then busy with the quilt. She was proud of what she had accomplished. It was going slowly, but she figured with more practice speed would come. Her stitches were becoming smaller and uniform. Every woman in gram's quilt guild wanted to have the smallest and most consistent stitches. It was a matter of pride among the women of the guild. Katie could remember gram talking about some of the ladies' stitches. The smaller the better when sewing the blocks together, they thought.

The next morning, just as she was getting out of the shower, the phone rang. Nick's mother said, "Katie, I am sorry to bother you, but I just wanted you to know we miss you being around nearly as much as we miss Nick. We would like for you to come for supper tonight after work. I thought you might like to pack some old comfortable clothes so you can come straight from work."

Katie was delighted with the invitation and accepted without hesitation, telling her future mother-in-law, "I'll be there shortly after five o'clock."

She was busy at the oil company office that day. There was always something happening with one of the many wells the operated, and the day passed quickly. Katie was looking forward to going to Nick's house to visit with his folks.

About four-thirty Nick called her at work. "Hi, hon. I got my phone hooked up. I guess you can tell, huh? My new phone number 618-934-4564."

"It is so good to hear from you, but I only have a minute. Got to get a few more things done before closing," Katie said.

"I won't keep you, but I love you Katie. How is it going with my favorite gal? You haven't changed your mind, have you?"

"No, you aren't getting out of this engagement that easy. How are your classes going?"

"I think my classes are going to be interesting. One may be a little bit of a struggle. I think it may take some major studying but I'm going to do okay."

"By the way, I do have a dinner date tonight and yes, there is a man involved. Hope you don't mind."

"Mind? I'm gone a couple of days and you have dinner plans with a man."

"That's right, a man, I'm going to your folks' house. They asked me for supper," she said, and threw in a chuckle.

"Well in that case I guess it is okay. Tell them all hello and give them my telephone number. I better let you go. I'm going to the library with some guys tonight. Love ya. Bye."

I truly am a lucky guy, he thought to himself, to have such a wonderful girl. As he started to study, he looked at the clock and thought of Katie eating supper with his folks. He could almost smell his mother's kitchen. It always had good smells wafting from it. He knew she would try to fix all of Katie's favorites, and he caught himself thinking of the menu his mom had planned.

What Nick didn't know was that when Katie got there,

supper hadn't been started. Nick's dad met her in the yard and said, "Katie, I needed a belt for the combine, and I sent Sue after it, but they were out of them. The dealership in the next town had one and she went over there to get it. Sue called and said she would be later in getting home and therefore supper is on hold. Just go on in, sit down and make yourself at home. I've got some things to finish up, and I'll be in shortly."

"Is there anything I can help you with out here?"

"No, I don't think so. Just go on inside. I'll be done here in a little while," Carl said.

Since there was nothing to do outside, Katie went in the house as Carl had suggested, but she wasn't about to sit down. Her mother had not raised her to just sit idly by and do nothing. There was a meal to prepare and she always enjoyed helping Nick's family if she could. They always seemed to appreciate anything she did. Katie looked around the kitchen and saw a box of spaghetti and a quart jar of Sue's home-canned sauce on the counter. Looking in the refrigerator, she saw a package of hamburger thawing, and figured this was what Sue was planning for supper. Coming from an Italian background, Katie knew how to prepare pasta the way it is supposed to be prepared, the real way. She remembered seeing freshly picked garden onions, peppers, and tomatoes on the porch. Assuming Sue planned to use these at some time and not let them go to waste, she diced and chopped some of them and started them simmering. Since Katie had been at the house many times before, she knew where most of the kitchen items were, so she had no problem finding pans and most of the spices she wanted to use. After mixing the fresh hamburger, spices, and crushed cracker crumbs together, she started shaping small meatballs and browning them in a skillet. Katie was going to make real Italian spaghetti, and that meant seasoned meatballs with fresh homemade sauce; not loose meat, browned and mixed with store-bought sauce.

When Sue got home from the implement store, Carl was just walking to the house at about the same time. She was hurrying because she knew she was running late with supper and Katie would be sitting in there waiting for them both. When they opened the back door, they could tell Katie had not been sitting. It smelled as if an Italian restaurant had moved in their kitchen.

Katie said, "I hope you don't mind me taking over your kitchen, but I couldn't see just sitting there and waiting for you, doing nothing. I thought I could at least start supper."

"If it tastes anything like it smells, you can come back and use my kitchen any time, any time at all," Sue was quick to assure her.

"Supper is almost ready to serve. You better get washed up," Katie remarked, as she and Sue finished the salad. Carl hurried to wash up and then helped set the table.

"I can't wait to get a plate of this spaghetti. I'm starved, and it smells wonderful," he said, as he kissed the end of his fingers and tried to emulate an Italian.

There was spaghetti, salad and garlic bread, and fresh lemonade to drink. Everything was delicious. They all had a good time visiting. Nick's parents enjoyed hearing about Katie's call from Nick. It was good to hear how he was excited about his classes.

Of course, no meal is complete at a farmhouse without some debate on the weather. After they covered that subject in depth, they discussed plans to start harvesting in a few weeks. Carl had been out testing the beans, and he thought the fields north of the house were a little closer to being ready to cut than some of the others. He had worked all day getting ready to start the harvest. He read the paper while Sue and Katie did the dishes.

"I better head home," Katie told them, "but call anytime if I can help do something. I'll be glad to come out and help. I'm looking forward to the weekend."

The weekend finally arrived. When Nick got home, he was eager to share all his news and experiences with Katie and his family. He told them every detail about school. It was good to have Nick home, but time for him to head back to school came all too fast.

The next week was busy but Katie tried hard each evening to work on the quilt. She was gaining a little each day and was proud of what she had accomplished.

She was always anxious to hear from Nick. Sometimes he would call or drop her a little note. He kept her posted on everything going on in school. On Thursday, she disappointedly heard from Nick, saying that he just didn't see how he could possibly make it home on Friday night as planned.

Katie could hear the excitement in Nick's voice, "There is an opportunity to work in the lab at school and earn extra credit, and I just can't pass up that chance. I really want to come home, but I think this is a good oportunity for me," Nick told Katie.

Fall harvest was just starting and Nick wanted to be there; however, he hoped everyone understood school was important too, and he was sure they did. He could remember when Mark went away to college. Their mother had always insisted Mark study and keep his grades up. This had left a lot of work for Nick and his dad, but they had made it through the busy seasons. He wished he could be in both places, college and helping on the farm, but sometimes life is not that simple.

Friday at work, Katie was feeling down because Nick

wasn't going to be home for the weekend. Katie always enjoyed being with Nick, even if it was nothing more than helping on the farm,. She had come to look forward to helping all she could on the farm. Katie didn't feel she had to be "taken out" to a movie or dinner all the time like some girls she knew.

About mid afternoon Katie answered the phone at work and found it was Nick's mom on the phone. Sue sounded terrible. "Katie, I was wondering if you could come out to the farm after work. I have caught this horrible cold, and Carl is wanting me to go to bed, but there are still some things that need done. I would just appreciate your help."

Katie assured her that she would be glad to come out and help all she could, but she was sorry to hear that she wasn't feeling well.

When Katie arrived at the farm after she got off work, she found Nick's brother, Mark, servicing the drill. "What are you doing, did you have trouble?" she asks.

"No, not really, just maintenance work. I just sent Anna after some more wheat seed. I didn't realize we were running that low. I thought there were several more bags in the shed, but I guess someone had loaded them on the truck and brought them to me. Therefore, I thought I would take this time to check over the drill. I hate to be planting wheat and have it break down. I do not like for anything to break down. It is better to grease it and check the settings and see that everything is working properly once in awhile. Preventative maintenance saves a lot of time in the end."

"I bet you are right. Have you got any idea what I can do to help? Your mom called and asked if I would come out after work, so I changed clothes before I left the office. I had some jeans in the car. Just tell me what to do."

"Well, Katie, I think dad wants you to come up to the

field north of the house and maybe relieve mom. She is feeling bad, but will not give up. You can take dad's pickup. They want you to make a few trips to the elevator in the grain truck if you don't care. I'm hoping to get this done and maybe eat a sandwich before Anna gets back. They just finished the field over by my grandparents' house and moved to the field north of here. There are still a couple wagons full of beans sitting over by Grandpa's we will need to get in the barn before the dew starts falling."

"Maybe I can talk your mom into laying down for awhile. She sounded awful on the phone."

"Well, good luck on that one!"

When she got to the field, she wasn't sure what had just happened. The combine was sitting "cock-eyed" as her grandpa would have said. She could see Carl and Sue standing there looking at it. This did not look good.

"What on earth happened?" she asked when she drove up.

"Oh, that little creek is notorious for overflowing its banks whenever there is a good rain, and we had several good rains last month. I should have checked on the bank here, it has washed out before, several years ago. I apparently drove over too close to the edge and when that front tire bounced in that gully, looks like that hopper of beans all shifted to one side. Guess that made just enough weight to cause the back of the combine to slide down the bank. I've got it marred down in that old gooey silt and mud now 'till I don't know how we will get it out. I sure hope it doesn't turn over. I'm almost afraid to breathe in that direction. Is Mark still at the house?"

"Yes, I just talked to him."

"Well, would you take Sue up to the house and tell her to go lay down, and tell Mark to bring the big tractor back down here and all those chains from the barn."

"No, I'm not going to the house till I see for sure you are all okay and the combine is out. Then I promise I'll go to the house," Sue said.

"You heard her, Katie. She's the boss. Just go get Mark if you would, please," Carl said.

She rushed back to the house. "Mark, you won't believe how the combine is sitting. Your dad said he is afraid to breathe in that direction, for fear it will turn over. It is stuck so deep, but teetering there on the creek bank. It is really in a terrible mess. He said to tell you to bring the big tractor and the chains from the barn, and, Mark, you better hurry."

"Is he hurt?" Mark asked, as he was already heading to the barn for the chains.

"No. He is okay, just shook up."

Mark was shocked when he saw the position the combine was sitting in. He shook his head. "I'm sure glad you got us in this mess instead of me, Dad. How did you keep it from going over in the creek? What happened anyway?"

"It looks like it really has washed a gully there. It's farther out in the field than I realized, and when I hit the gully and the weight shifted, well, you can see what happened. I just can't believe it is washed out this far into the field. We have to disk this up and sow grass seed to keep it from washing out any more," Carl said.

"Well, let's not worry about that right now. If we get the combine out without it turning over or tearing up something, we will be fortunate. I think we will have to shovel some of those beans out of the hopper, since the auger is on the side toward the creek. What do you think?"

"You are probably right, that is a lot of extra weight. I

thought we were so smart getting such a big hopper but right now it is a shame it isn't smaller," Carl said.

Katie noticed that Sue was shivering and her eyes were watering. Sue looked miserable. Katie told her to get in the pickup, and she turned up the heater. She reached over and felt of her forehead. Sue was burning up with fever, but having chills. Katie wanted to take her home, but Sue wouldn't hear of it, at least not until the combine was out and they were all safe.

"Have mom pull that big truck up here so I can shovel some of these beans in it," Mark yelled.

"She doesn't feel like it. She is in the pickup with the heater on, but I can get it," Katie said.

"I'll get the tractor and chain hooked up while you are shoveling," Carl said. "How do you think we can steady that thing so it don't go on over?"

"I'm not sure, Dad. Do you think we could hook the grain truck on to it somehow and hold it?"

"Hey, if I can help at all, I will, you will just have to tell me exactly what to do," Katie said. She felt inadequate, but she wanted to be of some assistance.

They hooked both the tractor and the grain truck to the combine and told Katie to pull slow and easy when they gave her the signal, and stay even with the tractor.

Katie was a little nervous and she was hoping she would do the right thing.

If the tractor could move the combine at all, they were hoping the grain truck would help to balance it. With a little luck and a quick prayer, they could keep the combine from slipping further into the creek and slowly pull it out onto dry, level ground.

It took several slow, agonizing tries. They would go forward a few inches and then have to get out and hook up the chains at a different angle, then pull again. At least six times Carl had to climb down from the combine and redo the chains from a different perspective. He and Mark had to keep hooking them at different angles and then pull a few more feet, always keeping the grain truck in line to keep the combine balanced.

Carl and Mark, covered in mud from head to toe, were trying to scrape it off their shoes on the steps of the combine and tractor before climbing in. The machinery was a mess, but they could be cleaned with the pressure hose at home. The mess from the mud was not a priority now.

At one point Carl jumped out of the cab of the combine waving both arms at Mark for him to stop, "We've got this combine in a bind. We have to let it go back down toward the creek a little bit, and get another pull on it. I'm afraid if you pull it any more, we will bend the frame. I can hear it! Mark, this is worse than I thought. We really got it in a predicament now! I'm afraid it is going to go over!"

"Hang on, Dad. Don't climb down, we'll get it." Mark was hurrying as fast as he could to readjust the chains. "Back up, Katie. I need to unhook your chain, too. Head your truck out that way a little more, not much."

As Mark headed back over to his tractor, he looked at Katie and said, "I think it is going to turn over, and Dad's in it. Don't let the clutch slip, Katie ."

Katie was nervous, what if she started too fast or did something wrong, "Please God, be with us all. Lend us a hand God and help me to do the right thing to assist Mark and Carl. Keep us all safe."

Mark, with Katie's help in the truck, was ultimately able to pull the combine to drier ground, where, finally, the combine could pull itself. It took over two hours to get the combine out of the mud and back safely on level, dry ground. Everyone finally breathed a sigh of relief, and a prayer of thanks.

"Katie, thanks for the help. I don't think the two of us could have done it." Carl said.

"I know we couldn't have done it," Mark said. "Wait 'till Nick hears how we broke you in while he was gone. He'll be proud of you, Katie ."

"I'm just glad I could help, and nothing tore up."

Mark took off for home on the tractor, and Katie went to check on Sue who was still in the pickup. She had parked it well out of the way in case anything unforeseen happened. Katie knew Sue would be very pleased that the combine was out. Everyone was safe and no equipment torn up. Sue always worried about Carl and the boys. Katie was somewhat surprised that Sue had not gotten out of the pickup to congratulate them for getting the combine out.

When she got to the truck, she found Sue sleeping. She was breathing hard and seemed to be tossing her head back and forth, not a restful, peaceful sleep at all. Her face, flushed and glowing, felt as though she was burning up when Katie felt her cheek and forehead. Katie was very concerned for her and wanted to get her to the house where she would be comfortable in her own bed, wrapped in a warm quilt.

She drove back over to the combine to see why Carl wasn't moving yet, to tell him that Sue's temperature had continued to rise, and ask him what doctor she could call to get something called into the pharmacy. She thought Carl was in the cab of the combine, but could not see from her seat inside the pickup truck. Katie got out of the truck to get his attention but she still couldn't see him in the combine. She called out, "Carl, where are you?" As she walked around the header of the combine, she found him. He was laying there on the ground with his leg caught in the bottom step and his shoulder wedged against the tire.

"Katie! Oh Katie, I'm so glad you are still here. I thought everyone was gone and I was here alone. Please go get Mark. My leg is broke, maybe my shoulder, too. Please hurry, Katie! It hurts so bad I can't stand it. You better go call an ambulance, too," Carl said.

Carl had big tears in his eyes, and he could not move. It broke Katie's heart to see him there, but she was afraid to try to move him, terrified that she would worsen the injury and increase pain.

"Hurry, Katie," she heard him say as she ran to the pickup.

She took off in the pickup racing to catch Mark who was ready to pull out on the road from the field. She was honking and blinking her lights as she flew to catch him.

Sue didn't even wake up. Katie was so worried, she knew Sue's temperature was soaring.

When Mark saw the pickup with the lights blinking, he stopped immediately. He knew something was wrong, but when he saw Katie, and the tears streaming down her face, he felt a twinge of panic pass through his body. Before she even opened her mouth, he knew it was serious.

"Your dad has slipped. He knows his leg is broken. He looks awful. Mark, he is really hurt. I'll go to the house to call an ambulance and be right back," she yelled over the tractor.

"Take me back to him first." He turned off the tractor and then jumped into the back of the truck. "Hurry, Katie! I'm holding on," he screamed at her.

She was barely even with the combine and not nearly stopped when he jumped over the side of the truck and hollered, "Go to the house and call an ambulance, Katie."

"Sue, I wish you would wake up," Katie said, as she

shook her arm. Katie was driving the pickup as fast as it would go across the field, rushing to get home to call the ambulance. Sue didn't answer or move, as Katie bounced her across the field. Katie couldn't help noticed how hot Sue's arm felt.

As Katie pulled in the driveway, Anna was walking up the steps to the back door. Katie shouted to her, "Call for an ambulance! Hurry! Please hurry! Carl is hurt and Sue is sick. They need it at the field just north of here."

Anna didn't ask any questions. She could tell by the tone of Katie's voice that something bad had happened. She ran in the house and called the ambulance and was heading out to the pickup when Katie, said, "Oh, we need a blanket for Sue. Do you have one in your truck? She is shivering! I think Sue needs to go to the hospital, too. Her fever is entirely too high." Anna quickly grabbed a crocheted afghan out of her pickup that she kept in there for the kids.

Anna's first question to Katie was, "Is Mark okay, Katie, is Mark okay?"

"Yes, he is with his dad."

Katie flipped down the driver's side seat so Anna could jump in the back seat of the super-cab pickup, since Sue was on the other side. Katie gunned the engine and they were immediately on their way back to the field.

"You won't believe all that has happened. Carl got the combine stuck and we pulled it out, then he slipped on the steps and his leg is broke and maybe his shoulder. He looked awful. There was so much mud caked on the steps, apparently when he was getting back in the combine, he slipped. They had tracked a lot of it on the steps when climbing in and out to reset the chains. He was in so much pain." Katie tried to fill her in quickly as they were on the way back to the field.

"I can't believe Sue is sleeping," Anna said.

"Feel of her head. She is burning up, but having cold chills. She needs to go to the hospital, too" Katie said.

"I feel terrible that you had to deal with all of this, but I'm sure glad you came when you did. Mark would have been beside himself. Well, I just don't know how he would have handled it all. Carl would have been left laying there if you hadn't gone back. I can't believe all that has taken place while I was gone. I don't know what would have happened without you here," Anna said. "I would have been back sooner, but there were several ahead of me at the elevator."

When the girls arrived at the combine, Mark was sitting on the ground holding his Dad's head. "How long will it be until the ambulance arrives?"

"Not long," Anna answered. "They said it would just be a few minutes. They happened to have one on this end of town, they would radio him to come on out here."

Please God, don't let it be long, she thought. Although Katie had tried to tell her how bad it was, she was not at all prepared for the scene before her. Carl was in terrible shape. Holding back the tears was not possible; Anna couldn't control herself. She had to step around to the other side of the combine for a moment to compose herself.

"I wanted to try to make him more comfortable, but I couldn't. He wanted me to try to get his leg out of the ladder. He thought it would feel better. The first time I moved it, he screamed so loud. I've never heard a human scream like that." Mark had to stop and wipe the tears away. "It was the most bloodcurdling sound I have ever heard. I couldn't move it any more, I moved back to his head and tried to hold him as best I could to relieve some of the strain on his shoulder. He just now drifted into a state of unconsciousness, as I held him. Anna, can you hold him here? I'll auger those beans out of the hopper. Dad wouldn't want them to get wet."

"I'll get the truck up here," Katie said.

They waited for what seemed like an eternity, but actually the ambulance arrived in just a short while from the time Anna had called.

The attendants could tell immediately that the leg was broken, and possibly in a couple places. After closer examination they told Mark that Carl's shoulder was dislocated. They were confident it was not broken. They first hooked him up to an I.V. with some medication in it and gave him a shot.

"This will help him bear some of the pain that he will endure when we move him, and put him into a deeper state of unconsciousness," one of the attendants told them.

It was probably a good thing Carl had passed out, because the attendants were very careful, but getting him on the stretcher was a job. Moving his leg and the shoulder would have caused unbearable pain. Even unconscious, he had still moaned several times, so loud the attendant had said, "Sorry. Sorry. We don't mean to hurt you. We're trying to help you, Carl."

"You've got to get his mom out of the truck," Anna said. "She's burning up with fever and I'm afraid she, too, has slipped into a very deep sleep. She wouldn't give up and go to the house earlier, now her temperature has skyrocketed."

They loaded both Mark's parents in the ambulance. Katie and Anna insisted Mark ride to the hospital with them, and they would follow shortly.

"Get all the wagons and trucks in the shed that you can, Dad's first concern would be the beans. Just do the best you can girls," Mark said as he was getting in the ambulance.

The ambulance, trying to take it easy, but still bouncing some as it made its way across the field, soon pulled out onto the road. The driver then turned on the siren, and proceeded to pick up speed on the oiled country road. Katie and Anna were still standing there, frozen, by the combine with their arms around each other. Their eyes were glued to the ambulance as it went over the hill and out of their sight, as tears welled up. They could still hear that eerie sound of the siren, that horrible eerie sound that brought a chill to the very center of their nervous systems.

They were too much in shock to say anything, standing there, as a new wave of tears rolled down both their faces. Both were sending up a silent prayer, the siren's wail sounding frightening as it headed for town.

This left Anna and Katie to get the trucks and wagons that were loaded with grain in the sheds before the rain hit. Thunderstorms, forecasted for later that evening, seemed to be rolling in from the south. The wind was picking up and the low rumble of thunder could be heard in the distance.

Chapter 13

"Nick! Oh, my, Anna. I just thought of Nick," Katie said. "Should I go call him or wait to see what we find out at the hospital?" How could she tell him all that had happened in one evening?

"Let's wait 'till we hear from Mark," Anna suggested. "Then we will hopefully have a little more information to pass on. Maybe it won't be as bad as we first thought. I really think that would be better. Besides, look at those clouds! We have to get this grain in before it gets wet, and it is getting dark."

Katie helped Anna all she could, but she wished she could do more. Anna even knew how to manage the tractors and wagons. Katie was impressed. She vowed, then and there, that she was going to learn how to handle the equipment. If she and Nick were to live on a farm, she realized, after tonight, that she needed to be able to handle things in case of an emergency. Besides, she wanted to be a valuable partner to Nick. She wanted him to be proud of her.

Katie could drive the trucks and help hook up the wagons. She also helped watch while Anna was backing them in the sheds and barn.

Anna and Katie decided as soon as they got everything put in the barns, they would go in the house and call Nick. Maybe by that time Mark would have left some word about his folks on the answering machine and they would have more to tell Nick.

The thunder in the distance was rumbling louder and louder. They were relieved when the last wagon was inside and the doors closed. Closing the big sliding shed doors had really been a challenge for the girls. The wind had picked up and it was hard to get the huge doors latched down.

"I'm sure glad Mark thought to auger the rest of the beans out of the combine hopper while he waited on the ambulance. I couldn't have taken care of the combine," Anna said.

It took about two hours to get everything put away in the barns. They were proud of themselves. When everything was in a shed or barn out of the weather, the girls headed for the house. The sky was alive with lightening back to the south, but they were hoping the rain would miss them this time, although it was getting closer and closer.

As they were walking in the house, the phone was ringing. They assumed it would be Mark, giving them some sort of update and checking to see how they were doing. Instead, it was Nick. When he heard Anna, he was surprised. In his cheerful tone of voice he asked, "How is my favorite sister-in-law?"

"We were just talking about calling you. Things are not real good here Nick. A lot has happened this evening. I hate to tell you. Your mom is so sick and has such a high temperature. She probably has pneumonia, but that is just Katie's and my diagnosis. In addition, Nick, your dad fell. He twisted his leg somehow in the steps on the combine and it is broken. The attendants on the ambulance said possibly in a couple of places. His shoulder is messed up, too, but we don't know how bad yet. They took them both to the hospital in the ambulance."

"Oh, no! Anna, how did all this happen? How bad are they? How did he fall?" Nick was firing questions at her.

"Well, your mom slept through the whole thing, her temperature was so high, so that should tell you something. She was in the pickup having chills, with the heater on full blast. You know she would have been right out there helping if she could have dragged herself out there. Seems as though your dad got the combine stuck and......it's a long story, and I wasn't here. Katie and Mark were in charge. Mark is at the hospital now with your folks and Katie helped me put away the machinery and beans."

"Is she there now?" Nick said.

"Yes, she's here. We are going to clean up and go to the hospital. Do you want to talk to her?"

"Well, no need really, and I need to get on my way. I'll just meet you guys there. I was coming home in the morning after all since there were some things cancelled. I will just start home now. I think I'll call the hospital first and see if I can talk with Mark and find something out about the folks. I'll see you guys in a few hours."

"Drive carefully, Nick. We need you here safe and sound," Anna said.

After hanging up the phone, he was in such a hurry he just grabbed some clothes and headed out the door. Calling the hospital would just take valuable minutes away from the time he could be on his way home. They would put him on hold 'till they found Mark, and he might not know much by now anyway, and he was too anxious to get home and be with the family to sit on hold for any length of time. He could find out the details and the severity of Carl's injuries first-hand when he got there.

He was worried about his folks and he knew that his dad would be out for the rest of the harvest season. He wanted desperately to be able to help in some way.

"Please, God, please let the folks be okay," he prayed aloud. He said that prayer over several times on the way home, also asking that God be with the doctors and guide them in the right paths to be able to help his parents recover fully. He loved both his parents so much, and wanted very much to be at the hospital.

The family did not like to work on Sunday; however, occasionally it was necessary and Nick figured this would definitely be one of those times. They would have to get as much done toward the harvest as possible this weekend. Hopefully, the weather would cooperate.

He found himself gripping the steering wheel tightly and his eyes were fasten to the road. God willing, the rain that was threatening would miss them. When his dad started coming around, Nick knew his first worry would be the farm.

He needed to be with Mark, and he knew Mark would need him. They had always been close. He couldn't imagine handling this situation without Mark beside him, so he wanted to be there to support Mark.

When Anna hung up, she turned to Katie. "He was in such a hurry to start for home that he said he would see you at the hospital. I hope he drives carefully. Let's go over to my house and shower. I'm sure I can find some clothes for you to put on."

Both girls were covered in mud and grease, and shivering from being in the damp night air. They were anxious to get in some dry clothes. Anna and Katie were about the same size and fast becoming close friends. After what they had been through tonight, they had made a close bond.

"A hot shower," Katie said. "Right now that sounds heavenly."

They checked Sue and Carl's house, closed the windows, locked the doors and jumped in Anna's truck and headed for her house. They really hated to take time for a shower, but they were so dirty and didn't know when they would get another chance. Consequently, they hurriedly showered and were ready to go to the hospital in record time.

"Mark would not believe we both got ready in such a short time," Anna said.

Once at the hospital, Katie and Anna found Mark in the waiting room with his head in his hands. He was so glad to see them. When he saw them coming in the room he stood up and hugged Anna as if she was his lifeline. He then did something out of character for Mark. He reached out and put his arm around Katie, too.

Once he got himself under control he asked, "Well, Katie, how do you like being part of our family? Trust me; it isn't usually quite this traumatic."

Katie smiled and looked at them both. "Thank you for including me as part of the family. I certainly hope every day isn't like today."

Mark proceeded to tell them everything he had learned so far. "The doctors took dad to surgery. The emergency room doctor called in a specialist, an orthopedic surgeon. Guess we are lucky to have him in our small town. They say he is one of the best in the state. They told me the leg is broken in two places and he needed surgery in order to set it correctly. It is really a bad injury and he is going to be out of commission for quite some time. They also said the shoulder is dislocated. It isn't broken, but the doctor said that it could possibly cause him a lot of trouble if it isn't taken care of properly. I wish Nick had been here, but there was really nothing else to do but sign the papers for them to go ahead with the surgery.

"Mom, on the other hand, does, in fact, have pneumonia. They gave her a couple of shots and started her on antibiotics. She woke up briefly but I didn't try to tell her anything that had happened. That would have been too much for her, and there will be plenty of time to tell her later, when she is feeling stronger.

The doctor wanted her to rest and one of the shots had been to relax her, so she went back to sleep shortly after waking. Thinking all was well at home, and all she needed to do was rest, she drifted back to sleep. She was very weak, barely spoke in a whisper, and mentioned something about Dad putting all the grain away. She asked if the combine was out. I told her it was, and she closed her eyes.

"Well, now that I've given you the scoop on what is happening here, what have you two girls been up to?"

"Oh, we've been loungin' around, takin' it easy for the last couple hours," Anna told him and smiled.

"Believe that and I'll sell ya the Golden Gate Bridge," Katie put in with a big smile on her face.

"Let's see. I called my folks and they are keeping the girls till further notice. Katie and I got all the wagons and trucks in the shed down on the old Eubank place and in the barn at the house. I couldn't have done it by myself. Katie and I work good together. Cassie and Jodi wanted me to tell you they wanted to do something to help, and Mom said she would call Mary Norma and get the prayer chain started. I talked to Nick and he is on his way home. I'd say he should be here in a few hours, wouldn't you, Katie?"

"Or less, if I know him, I hope he doesn't get in too big a hurry!"

There was nothing else to do but sit and wait now. Wait on Nick to arrive and wait on the doctors to come out and tell them what had happened in surgery. Most importantly, they needed to pray for strength for what was to come, and to thank God for his blessings so far. The accident could have been so much worse. They really were blessed in so many ways. They joined hands, bowed their heads, and each said a prayer asking for God's help and guidance.

They sat together, rehashed the accident and read every newspaper in the waiting room. Finally, Katie said, "I'm hungry. How about you? Would you guys like a sandwich? I'll go get them if you don't mind me using your car."

Anna and Mark, for the first time realized how hungry they were, and Anna said, "If you can handle Carl's trucks, you can surely drive my car. I'll take a super-sized sandwich, a large order of fries and a forty-four-ounce soda."

Mark just looked at her and shook his head. He asked, "Can I have something, or were you planning on eating enough for me, too?"

As soon as those words were out of his mouth, he started to smile. "That reminds me, you haven't told me how the doctor's appointment went this morning."

Anna just smiled that secret smile husbands and wives have between themselves, and Mark knew. He scooped her up in his arms and hugged her and planted kisses all over her face. "I guess I gave myself away by ordering so much to eat, didn't I? I'm really starved."

By that time, grinning from ear to ear, Katie figured out what was going on. "Is there some bit of news you haven't told yet? Is there anything you want to share, or is this a private moment?" They all hugged again, this time a more joyful hug, for the new life God was going to give to their family.

That is the way Nick found them, hugging and crying, when he walked into the waiting room of the hospital. Tentatively, he asked, "Is this a good family hug or a bad family hug? I don't know whether I should be more alarmed than I already am or what to think."

Katie grabbed him and they included him in the hug, too. Another round of tears and smiles erupted and this baffled Nick even more. "It's going to be okay, Nick," Katie said. "Especially now that we are all here and you are safe. It is going to be okay." She hugged him so hard.

Anna said, "This isn't exactly how or where I planned to tell the family this news, but, Nick, you are going to be an uncle again."

"Congratulations about the baby. I'm really happy for you, but please tell me about the folks. How are they? Are they going to be all right?"

Nick was excited about the baby, but he was so worried about his folks. and he was glad to be home, too. Nick just wasn't sure what emotion to express, or how to express it.

Mark hugged Nick, "I'm glad you are here little brother. I need you."

"Believe me, I needed to be here, too," Nick sighed. "You can't imagine, it was the longest trip ever, and I couldn't go any faster because of the rain and because your wife told me to drive carefully, so it is her fault!"

Everyone seemed to talk at once, but little by little, Nick felt he knew what was going on.

"You want to go down and look in on mom?" Mark asked. "I'll go with you."

"Sure, let's go," Nick said.

After Nick had seen his parents and had all the details, he felt a little calmer. They once again remembered they had not eaten. Katie and Nick volunteered to go for the food. They especially didn't want Anna to be hungry, now that she was eating for two.

Katie said, "I know Sue will be thrilled when she hears there will be a new baby in the family."

"She will be thrilled, won't she?" Mark said.

"We will all go out to celebrate the new baby, when everyone gets to feeling better and the combining is done," Nick said.

"The way dad looked, the baby may be seventeen before we get everyone on their feet again. Nick, you have never seen anything like it, has he Katie ?" Mark said.

"No, you can't imagine, and I don't ever want to see anyone in that much pain again as long as I live," Katie said.

"Katie tried to warn me, but when I got there, at first sight of him I had to go around on the other side of the combine and get myself in control, and I thought I was going to throw up," Anna said.

"If I would have known you were pregnant I wouldn't have taken you back down there. It's a wonder you didn't get sick," Katie said.

"I bet your grandma would have had an old saying about that," Nick said, having heard Katie many times refer to Grandma's old saying.

"Oh, definitely, she had one for everything."

As they were walking out to the car, Nick said, "I would have been here sooner, but there were places I could hardly see where I was going it was raining so hard. Luckily I drove out of it several miles back. Hopefully our farm didn't get the downfall I drove through. If it did, it will be a week before anyone can get into the fields."

"The thunder and lightning isn't near as bad as it was when Anna and I came into town," Katie told him. Then she started to laugh.

"What is the matter with you?"

"I can't help thinking, we are beginning to sound like

your folks, having a conversation about the weather," Katie said.

"You are right, but I really hope it misses us so I can help Mark get some stuff done tomorrow," Nick said.

Katie tried to remember all the details of the evening. She told and retold Nick how his dad looked laying on the ground when she found him, as she tried to answer all Nick's many questions. She explained how the ambulance had come to the field and how much pain Carl endured. Nick winced as if he felt his pain, and slowly shook his head.

"Nick, Carl was as white as a ghost when they loaded him in the ambulance. All the time your mom was asleep in the pickup with the heater full blast. I tried to help Mark and your dad get the combine out, and we thought everything was going good until your dad slipped. It was awful to see him lying there," Katie said, as her voice started to crack once again.

"I can't imagine," Nick said, "and maybe I don't want to."

"I attempted to help Anna get the trucks and wagons in the sheds, and she even bragged to Mark that she would have never got it all done without me. She probably would have, she can handle that stuff, but it was nice of her to say I was a big help. She just seemed to know what to do and how to do it." Katie said.

"Well, Anna grew up on a farm, she has been doing this sort of thing all her life. So don't be disappointed if you can't back a wagon or trailer overnight. It takes a while to learn all this stuff. However, I'm proud of you, very proud of you. And if I know Anna, she wouldn't have bragged on you if she didn't mean it."

When they got back to the hospital with the food, everyone was quiet while they ate. When they were satisfied, they all chuckled at how much Anna ate. This rather relieved the tension. Katie told them how her grandma always said, "You always feel better with food in your stomach. It is God's nourishment for the soul, or something like that she used to say. She had so many sayings I can't remember them all exactly like she would have said them. Gram started every saying with 'Ma al'us said,' and then she proceeded with the old-time saying. She had a million of them."

The doctor came out to talk to them shortly after they finished eating. They were so glad to see him. It had been a very long wait. He told them that they had done a lot of extensive repairs to Carl's leg. He sat down with them in the waiting room and began to explain what all they had done. "It was broken in two places. The upper femur is fractured close to his hip. He was fortunate that it wasn't high enough to damage his hip joint. He also has a tib-fib fracture, which means both bones below the knee are broken, and these were, unfortunately, not clean breaks. It will be six to eight weeks before he will be able to bear weight on this leg.

"Now, in a few days we will start therapy. He will first have to learn how to roll over in bed with the weight of this cast without straining his leg. Even the easiest things will have to be learned because of the weight of the cast. It will really make a difference in his sense of balance and equilibrium. He will even have to learn to sit on the side of the bed correctly. Keep in mind that your dad will be in a cast from the hip to the ankle, this will be a lot of weight to carry around, and he will not be able to bend his leg at the knee.

Before he leaves the hospital, he will be put through a series of gait-training sessions. This is where the therapist will actually train him to walk again. He will learn to stand with a walker and he will have to be able to ambulate with either a walker or crutches before he leaves the hospital. There will be months of therapy to follow and a long recuperation time for his leg to heal properly.

In addition, there is a good chance that in a few months we might need to go back in for some more constructive surgery. I think it would be a good idea if one person stays all night with him and is here to push the medication pump when needed. This will keep him from getting into more pain than is necessary.

I know I have given you a lot of information to grasp at one time, but if you have any questions, feel free to ask. And you may not be able to think of any now but I'm sure later you will think of things you want to ask. Just make a note of them and I'll be glad to answer any questions you may have. I usually do my rounds between nine and eleven every morning." The doctor then stood to leave.

"Thank you so much," Mark said, as he shook his hand. "We appreciate all you have done."

Katie spoke up and said, "Now, I can spend the night for you guys. You all need to get some rest. Nick, you and Mark will need to get some sleep so you can work tomorrow, and Anna you and the baby need to get some rest too."

"That sounds okay to me. She is probably right, you know," Mark said to the others.

"Are you sure you don't mind? I hate to leave you up here by yourself," Nick said.

"I insist. It is the least I can do," Katie said.

As they were walking down the hall to leave, Mark said to Nick, "Dad is not going to be a very happy farmer. I don't know if he will be a very good patient, he has never been down for any length of time. Mom is going to have her hands full, and she has a long way to go to get her strength back."

After all the thunder and lightening, it looked like the rain was going to miss them. They would probably be able to get in the fields tomorrow.

Chapter 14

The night vigil started out favorably. Carl was resting and Katie made sure she was there at the bedside to push the morphine pump every time the timer allowed, so that he would not be in pain. The doctor had suggested that someone do this for him for the first 24 hours, at least. In between times, she would walk down to check on Sue, who was also sleeping. The medicine had really put her out.

At 2 o'clock Katie noticed that Sue was breathing differently and she became concerned. She called the nurse and they discovered that her temperature had risen two degrees in the last hour. This was not a good sign at all. The nurse called the doctor and he gave orders to increase the medication in the I.V. and give Sue a shot, which she did immediately.

Katie wondered about calling Nick, but decided she would give the medicine a chance and see what happened within the next hour. She paced the halls of the hospital and checked on both parents every fifteen minutes.

While she was sitting beside Sue's bed, Sue began to cough. It was as if she had so much obstruction in her throat and she needed to get it up. She started to gasp for air. Katie immediately rang for the nurse. Sue continued to cough and gasp. The nurse grabbed her, sat her up, and another nurse put a suction tube down her throat to suction the congestion out of her throat. Sue woke briefly as they were doing the procedure and tried to push them away. It seemed as though she hated the apparatus they had stuck down her throat.

After they had her calmed back down and breathing regularly, the nurses went back to the station, and Sue took Katie's hand. Sue whispered, "Please don't let them do that to me again. It hurt terribly."

The nurse told Katie that Sue's temperature was beginning to drop. The medicine must be working. Relieved to hear this news, at four o'clock she decided to go to the cafeteria for some hot chocolate. When she came back to the waiting room, she was both surprised and very glad to see Nick.

"What are you doing here?" she asked.

"I couldn't sleep; I worried about my folks and about you up here with them and what if something went wrong. All I could do was toss and turn. I decided it was time to run up here and see for myself how everyone was, and then I will go home and get busy. Where were you?"

"Well, I ran down to get a cup of hot chocolate. Thought it would feel warm and would revive me."

"I figured you were either there or in the bathroom, so I decided to sit and wait. I knew you would return."

Katie proceeded to tell him how the night had gone, and how his mother's temperature had gone up but then started back down after the increase in medicine. His father continued to rest with the help of the painkiller. She had to admit it was very comforting to have Nick there with her and his strong arm laid carelessly around her shoulders.

"Your mom got choked one time and I was so scared. The nurse put some sort of suction thing down her throat. Nick, it was awful. She took my hand and pulled me close to her so she could whisper to me, begging me not to let them do that again to her. That was when I had to go down the hall and wipe my eyes."

At 5:30 Nick said, "I better get home and help Mark with the milking and then we can get the machinery ready to go and be ready to start when the beans are dry enough to cut. I'll call my Aunt. She will want to come and help. She and mom are close. She will relieve you."

"I could probably use a nap," Katie admitted. "Be sure to tell her to bring a sweater."

They decided to check on them both before Nick left, and his mother was beginning to rouse a little as they walked in the room. They asked what they could do for her and how she was feeling. She couldn't remember how she had gotten to the hospital or what had happened at all. They didn't tell her all that had happened the evening before; they knew that she would worry about Carl. Nick suggested to Katie that it might be better to wait until up in the day and maybe even the doctor would want to tell her about Carl's incident. She was awake for a short time before drifting back to sleep.

It was a little after seven o'clock when a tall woman walked in the waiting room. Almost at once Katie knew she was there to sit with Sue. Katie couldn't believe how much she resembled her sister. They were definitely identical twins.

"Hi, you must be Katie. Nick said you would be the prettiest girl in here."

"I'm the only girl in here," Katie said, and they laughed.

I'm Nick's Aunt Lou Ann, Sue's twin sister. I can't

believe all that has taken place in the last twenty-four hours, can you? Nick asked if I would care to come up and relieve you. Sue and I have always been really close, so I'm here to help out. I would do anything for my sister, as I know she would do for me and my family. Now, you be sure and tell those boys if they need anything to call me. My family will do whatever we can to help out."

"Thank you for coming. I could tell you looked like Sue. I've heard her speak of you and it is nice to meet you, but I sure wish it was under better circumstances. It is unbelievable, that they are both in the hospital at the same time," Katie said.

Katie told her what was going on with both of them, and she mentioned that they had not yet told Sue about Carl being down the hall. Carl was still resting, so Katie told her what she had been doing all through the night.

"Well, thank you for staying, Katie. I know you are worn out and need to get home and get some sleep. Nick suggested the doctor tell Sue about Carl and I agree. When he comes in to check on her, I'll let him tell her, if she is awake. You know, she is really going to have to take care of herself because she will need all her strength to take care of Carl when he gets home from the hospital. I plan to come help her all I can. If you will just tell me where the coffee can be found I'll make out just fine."

Chapter 15

Katie would have loved to go by Nick's to see what was going on, but she had been awake all night and knew she needed to go home. She was in need of a shower and a nap. She went on to her house and it felt good to be home and among her own things. This house still did not seem like home, but it was where all her things were, and it was beginning to take on a cozy atmosphere. She missed the big house she had always loved, but surprisingly enough she was beginning to feel comfortable here.

After she called her folks to let them know about Sue and Carl, she took a quick shower. She then snuggled down into bed under her favorite quilt and said a prayer, asking God to look after Nick and his family. She also thanked him for looking after them all through the night.

She slept soundly for about six hours, and felt rested when she woke. She threw on some jeans and decided it might be wise to toss in some extra clothes for a quick change in case she needed them later. As she had learned, one never knew what was going to happen out on the farm.

The driveway was full of trucks when she arrived at the

farm. She went in the house to see if anyone was around. She hadn't noticed that the black pickup was her dad's.

"What is going on here?" Katie asked.

"Everyone in the neighborhood came in to help and so did your dad. Some brought equipment and trucks and some just came to see if they could help. Every farm around is represented here," Anna said.

The news of Carl's accident had traveled fast throughout this little Christian community. "This is just the way things are done around there. If someone is in need, the neighborhood chips in and tries to help," someone told her.

The men were all in the fields and the women were in the house fixing supper. The counter was full of cakes and pies and she could smell the hams in the oven. Instantly Katie was reminded she hadn't had anything to eat since the night before. "Could I maybe help out by sampling something? I'm famished."

She was so pleased that her folks had come in to help, too. Mom had brought more than her fair share of food, all Katie's favorites, including her famous fruit bar cookies. She knew her dad would be helpful. He was so handy with machinery.

Some of these men were like Nick and his family, they were just starting on their own crops, but this is the day they set aside to help a family in need.

Nick was in charge of the combining, and Mark was in charge of drilling the wheat. There was help for both jobs.

It was amazing. They would just move in to one field and stagger the combines and they would have a field cut in no time. The men disking and drilling wheat moved in the fields when the combines pulled out.

Nick and Mark had been in on helping the neighbors when someone was sick, but they never dreamed that everyone would show up that morning and help them. Their dad had always made sure he was right there if one of the neighbors needed anything. After the boys were old enough, sometimes he would send one of them, with a truck or wagon.

Later Nick told Katie , "One time dad took the combine and I went with him with our grain truck to help a family. The man had been in a car accident. A storm was forecast for the next day, but dad said, 'Boys, we need to help this family. Since the breadwinner of the family is down and out, they can't afford to loose this crop. We have to help them get it out of the fields, and worry about ours later.' So, we went over there, and everyone was there, just like today. The storm missed us and we were able to finish our crops in the next couple of days. Dad never let us forget that. He told us many times that God had provided time for us to finish our crops because we had helped out someone in need. Never miss helping your friends and neighbors. You never know when you might need help. God uses us to take care of those in need. God seems to use people for his purpose, helping someone in need, and having the favor returned tenfold."

Nearly every person there had a story to tell about how Carl had helped them at some time through the years, and now they wanted to repay him.

Late afternoon the women took all the food to the fields and they had a tailgate party, but it took several tailgates. They all joined hands making a big circle and the deacon of the small church down the road gave the blessing.

The food was delicious. Everyone agreed it was good to get together and work. They hated it that Carl and Sue were in the hospital and that was the reason they had gotten together. While they were eating dessert and finishing up,

Sue's sister came by the field. She said, "The doctor came in and he told Sue about Carl's accident. He said Sue was doing better, and Carl was doing as well as possible. He was beginning to come around more just before I left the hospital. Carl's sister came by and said she would be glad to sit for several hours. Now, don't you kids worry about a sitter. There are enough retired brothers and sisters to sit, and you young people just worry about getting the crops out of the fields."

Most of the men either had work in their own fields or outside jobs, and some of the younger ones had to be in school on Monday. Of course, they would all go to church in the morning. Katie's dad said he would love to help Mark, and insisted that Nick go back to college Sunday afternoon. Katie said she had some vacation time coming and could take a few days and help, too.

After everyone had gone home and the family cleaned up a little, they all went together to see how Carl and Sue were doing. Sue was sitting in a wheelchair in Carl's room, reassuring him that the boys were taking care of things, and she was sure with God's help everything would work out for the good. "After all, doesn't it say in the Bible that God uses all things good or bad to work for the good in the end?" she said.

Sue had begged the nurse to allow her to go see Carl, and she had cried when they told her no. So the doctor finally had relented, cautioning her to wear a mask and only stay a few minutes, so as not to wear out either patient. He had known the family for years and realized that Sue would not rest till she had seen her husband.

Carl was sort of in and out, the painkiller helping him to doze. He said he agreed with her, but it was hard to be lying on your back in the hospital when there was so much needing done and requiring his attention at home. Just then, he looked up and saw four smiling faces coming in the door.

Mark and Nick started talking at once telling Carl about all the good help they had during the day. They recounted how many acres they had combined and what all had happened during the day. Carl couldn't believe it. "Wait a minute, you are both talking so fast, I want to hear it all. Slow down and tell me one at a time."

Anna and Katie were excited to tell Sue about all the food and help they had from the women, too. Sue gave a faint smile "Isn't that wonderful! You girls make a list of everyone that was there. I want to write a note to each of them and thank them. Don't forget any of the details. You tell me all about it again in a few days. I feel so weak right now, and I'm afraid I probably need to go back and lay down."

The nurse came in about that time to take her back to bed. She admitted she needed to lie down.

Everyone could tell an improvement in Carl by the time they left to go home. He had tears in his eyes, just thinking about everyone coming to help him. He was so thankful. Sue suggested they all join hands and thank God for such wonderful friends and neighbors before the nurse took her back to her room. The nurse even joined hands with them and listened to the prayer.

Monday morning arrived and Katie and her dad reported to work bright and early. Nick had gone back to school and Mark said Anna would be down when she got the girls off to school.

They all four worked together well, discovering they made quite a team. With Nick coming home on weekends, they might make it through another harvest after all.

Sue was finally home after a week. Cassie and Jodi enjoyed helping take care of her. Katie made them nurses' hats out of folded newspaper, and they were so proud that they were helping, too. The girls saved Katie and Anna many steps, and were eager to help, especially where grandma was concerned.

Because Sue knew she needed to be as healthy and strong as possible when Carl came home, she tried to take care of herself and do as the doctor had suggested. She would need all her strength to take care of him when he was released from the hospital.

They all worked hard, and before long the end was in sight. It was hard for Carl, being in the hospital, when so much was going on at home. But the biggest struggle for him was learning how to maneuver the cast. They kept him busy at the hospital, with rehab most of the time. When he wasn't in rehabilitation he was resting, totally exhausted. He was beginning to wonder if he would ever regain his strength. He was just learning how to handle the cast, and it didn't take much to wear him out these days.

Carl was ecstatic when the day finally came for him to go home. It was a Saturday and Nick was home from school, so both boys and their mother came to the hospital to take Carl home.

Chapter 16

As the woods began to loose their fall colors and the temperatures began to drop, Carl could tell he was not improving nearly as rapidly as he had hoped. As the leaves were falling, so were Carl's spirits. He tried so hard to be a cheerful patient, and he disliked causing Sue any extra work. Finally, one morning as they were having coffee, he said to Sue, "I don't want to do this, but I think you will have to call the doctor today and see if we can get in. My leg has been hurting the last few days more and more, and it is not letting up. I don't want to go in, but he is going to have to do something. I'm not getting any better."

As soon as the office opened, Sue called. The office girl told her to come in as soon as they could and the doctor would look at him.

Sue then called Mark. "Do you have time to come help me take your dad to the doctor? He is in a lot of pain."

"What do you mean do I have time? Of course I have time for that. When do you want me there?"

"They said to bring him on in when we could get around."

"I'll be right there, Mom," Mark said.

Mark could tell his dad was in a lot of pain when he got there. His dad always smiled when he came in the back door, but today there was no smile. Mark had to help him get out to the car and then into the doctor's office.

The doctor soon came in and asked Carl several questions. After jotting down several notes, he said, "I worry about DVT occurring when I have a patient with a cast this size. Have you been doing the ankle pumps as frequently as we suggested?"

"Well, I've tried," Carl said.

"Lately, Doctor, it has been harder to get Carl to really do them correctly," Sue put in.

"I'm sorry, Doctor, I wanted to do as you said, but lately, I just haven't felt like exerting any energy at all."

I think I will call the hospital and reserve a room for you. You can go on over there. I'll order some x-rays, and do some blood tests. It looks as though you are running a temperature. We will check your white blood cell count. If it is elevated, along with the slight temperature you are running, I'm suspecting maybe you have a low-grade infection at the surgical site."

"What do those initials stand for that you mentioned earlier?" Carl asked.

"DVT, that stands for deep vein thrombosis, a blood clot, in layman's terms. We can't let that happen. If you do have a clot we have to get it dissolved before it moves. The ankle pumps help to stimulate blood flow, and the idea behind that exercise is to prevent blood clots, which can be fatal."

"I didn't realize the ankle pumps were that important. I have felt so awful for the last few days I just didn't have the energy to do those."

"We will take care of that. First, we will look at the

x-rays, see how the leg is healing, and have a look at the alignment. We will check for infection and any kind of clot, and probably put you on an antibiotic. Your blood pressure is slightly higher than usual, too, but you are under some stress, so that doesn't surprise me. I'll put you on some calan for that and we will get you lined out again. I don't guess I'll have to tell you to do those ankle exercises religiously after this will I?"

"If I can get to feeling better, I will do them just like you said," Carl said. "What time do you want me in the hospital?"

"I'll call over there now and give the order for you a room and have them schedule your x-rays, and they will give you a shot to reduce the infection and for the pain as soon as you get there."

"I'm ready to go. I feel awful. I'm ready for some help," Carl said.

Mark and Sue took him directly to the hospital. While he was resting, waiting for the x-rays, Sue and Mark went home to pick up some of his personal items.

The x-rays did show a very small blood clot and the doctors inserted a small screen, so in case the clot moved, it couldn't go up to the lungs or heart. Carl was hooked up to an I.V. immediately and antibiotics were administrated to take care of the infection. After several rounds of antibiotics and some helpful therapy, Carl told Sue, "I feel so much better and I can face living with his cast if it just doesn't hurt so badly. If this starts hurting again, I'm coming in immediately."

The doctor walked into the room just in time to hear Carl. "We are hoping you don't have any more problems," the doctor told him.

On Friday, the doctor told Carl he could go home the next morning, so Mark and Nick both came to help Sue bring Carl home from the hospital, again. They had to help Carl up the three steps into the house, once they were there.

"You can't imagine how good this old house looks. It makes me feel safe and secure, and that bed is begging me to come lay down in it," Carl said as they got up the steps and into the kitchen.

After the boys helped him into the bedroom and he was comfortably lying down in his own bed, the boys and Sue had a cup of coffee and talked for at least an hour or so.

Nick said, "You know, dad's right. When I come home from school this house does welcome me, along with the family. It shelters us and keeps us dry and warm. It holds so many memories. I hadn't really thought about it that way. We could always find another house if we had to, as long as the family was okay, but, you know, this house is really a big part of our family."

Mark laughed. "You're right! Remember all the Christmas trees and all those decorations that dad likes to put out? Remember the time you fell in the basement, but it was okay because you landed on your head. It's a wonder you didn't hurt the basement floor! Then the first time Cassie took a step, she was right over there, and she walked to dad. All the Easter egg hunts we have had, and remember the family reunions we've had here? So many things have happened in this house."

By this time Nick was chuckling. "Do you remember the time, Mark, that kid came home from school with you and was stranded for three days because of the snow? We have had a lot of fun here. I guess that is how Katie felt about that house of her grandpa's. I had never thought too much about it. I thought she just liked it because it was attractive, big, and cozy. She loved it because it holds a big part of her life. All the stories she has told me that happened both before and after she was born, and growing up. I guess I was maybe a little inconsiderate about how she felt. Now to see it going down-hill after she and her dad worked so hard is very sad. I would hate to see this place going to ruins."

Chapter 17

Christmas was one of Carl's favorite times of the year. He always decorated the outside of the house so it could be seen for miles around. This was a yearly, family event, just like celebrating everyones' birthdays. They always celebrated Carl's birthday and decorated for Christmas the day after Thanksgiving. Very few years had this family tradition been broken. In fact, the only time Nick could remember was the year his Grandma Neezy died. This year Carl just was not able to do any decorating. He would miss all that.

Carl enjoyed the small children's faces when they would get out of the cars to walk around and look at the decorations. Everyone drove out to Carl and Sue's to look at the lights. There were always many cars going by the house at night during the month of December, to view the Christmas decorations.

Mark had gone to Anna's family on Thanksgiving and Nick had gone to Katie's. Carl had missed their big family get-together. It was a long day for him.

He noticed Sue didn't say a whole lot about the kids not coming around, and that sort of surprised him. She did bake a couple pies in the afternoon and said, "Someone might come by tomorrow and I want to have something to offer them."

Bright and early on the following morning, Sue was up humming Christmas carols as she busied herself around the kitchen. "I think I'll put on a pot of green beans," she told Carl.

"That sounds pretty good." As he watched, she opened four quarts of her home-canned green beans and poured them into her favorite pan.

Sue didn't open her canned goods for every-day eating. She usually saved it for special gatherings. So when she opened four quarts, he began to get a little suspicious.

"Yeah, maybe someone will come see us old crippled folks." He smiled as he looked up at Sue. "We sure won't be decorating for Christmas this year."

"You mean you aren't going to climb the ladder with that cast on? I didn't think anything would keep you from decorating for Christmas," Sue said.

"Probably no ladder for me today, unless you want me back in the hospital again."

He sat in the old wooden rocker by his favorite kitchen window, with his leg propped up on a little stool. He could see about a quarter mile down the road to the corner. There he noticed four cars coming down the road toward their house. That was a lot of traffic for their country road in the middle of the day. They all were probably going somewhere together he surmised. Then he recognized Nick's car.

Nick pulled in the driveway and the other cars followed right behind him. "What's going on here?" Carl asked.

"Oh, I don't know, why?" Sue said with a big smile.

"You opened four quarts of green beans, four cars just pulled in the driveway, and you are smiling from ear to ear," he said with a grin on his face. He knew something was up, and since it was his birthday, he couldn't wait to find out what was taking place.

By that time, they were all coming in the back door with lots of food. Everyone was carrying a couple of dishes.

It was a beautiful cool crisp day for late November. "Is someone going to tell me what is going on?" Carl asked.

Nick looked at his dad and asked, "What do we always do the Friday after Thanksgiving? We have done it every year since I can remember."

"I know, but I'm just not able this year. Do you think I could climb a ladder with this walker and in a cast?" Carl asked. "What were you planning, to video the whole operation and send it in to that TV show?"

"Well, now, there is an idea. We hadn't thought of that one. We aren't really that cruel," Nick answered.

"Christmas decorating is really the reason we're all here. Anna and Katie's folks wanted to help too, so we are going to put you in a lounge chair in the yard to supervise. You can completely oversee the operation. Then we are going to have a birthday dinner. This is our birthday present to you, from all of us. Do you want us to sing first or just start decorating?" Mark asked.

Carl laughed. "Just decorate. I've heard you sing before, son. I can't believe you would all do this for me. Whose idea was this anyway?"

Mark said, "I think Anna and Katie cooked this up. You will have to blame them."

"Blame them! I want to thank them and all the rest of you for coming, too. But you don't have to do all the decorations, that is too much," Carl told them.

"Hey, we even brought extra. Anna found some decorations at an auction last week and that is what got all this in motion. Wait until you see what she got for you,"

Mark said. He knew his dad would be happy with what Anna had bought at the auction.

"Come on Grandpa, we get to help this year," Cassie said as she took Carl by the hand.

"Wait a minute, Honey. Grandpa needs his walker and I don't move too fast anymore," Carl told Cassie.

"Grandpa, can I help get the Santa and sleigh out this year?" Jodi inquired.

The boys assisted Carl down the steps and got him seated in the chaise lounge outside. Sue covered him with the heavy flannel "Cabin in the Woods" quilt and made sure he was warm enough. They all sang Christmas carols at the top of their lungs and had a wonderful time putting up the decorations.

By early afternoon, the temperature was beginning to drop and the decorating was coming together. It all looked so nice and everyone agreed they couldn't wait till dark to see how it all looked.

As the sun lowered in the western sky to a beautiful bright orange and purple sunset, everyone anxiously awaited darkness and the moment grandpa's Christmas lights came to life for the first time of the season.

Nick and Mark had many stories to tell about the "grand lighting" as it was known to the family. This year the boys took extra precautions to make sure the lights all came on without a hitch.

Meanwhile, it was time to eat and celebrate Carl's birthday. Carl almost broke down as he said the prayer, thanking God once again for everyone at the table and for all they had done for him.

Before everyone took their first bite, Jodi asked excitedly, for about the tenth time, "Is it dark enough to turn on the lights, Grandpa?"

"Let's turn the switch on boys! I think it is dark enough," Carl commanded.

"Drum roll, please," Mark said, as Nick went into the garage to turn on the lights.

Everyone ooohed and ahhhed and insisted that the part they helped decorate was the prettiest. Finally, Sue insisted that the food would be getting cold and they needed to eat.

"I'm a very lucky man," Carl said, "to be blessed with such a loving family and wonderful friends. The lights are spectacular; I think maybe it is better this year because Cassie and Jodi helped. Maybe we had better have them help every year from now on. What do you think Mark?"

"I don't see how we could do it without them anymore," Mark said.

"It is supposed to snow an inch or so tomorrow," Sue said. "It really will be breathtaking then."

"Snow. I can't believe it, today was so nice. That is just like the weather in Southern Illinois. It can change quickly, and my leg is aching a little tonight, always a sign of a change in the weather, the old timers used to say. My grandma could always forecast a change in the weather by how her back felt. Maybe that is how I will be with my leg. I sure hope not," Carl added.

The snow started falling Saturday afternoon. Enormous fat fluffy flakes drifted slowly to the ground not making a sound, giving everything a beautiful white blanket.

"I've always liked snow, especially if I was on the inside looking out. It makes everything look so clean and fresh. I guess it is God's way of covering the ugly," Sue said.

"You better get my jacket and help me outside," Carl responded. "If it covers the ugly, I should probably be out there, but it may take several inches and a couple of hours to get me covered completely!"

They both laughed together and Sue gave him a big hug. "I think your sense of humor is the reason I fell in love with you. And I thank God that I did. We have such a wonderful family and friends."

Chapter 18

On Carl's next visit to the doctor's office to check his leg, he got a good report and it looked to be healing nicely. "Carl, I'd say you have another five weeks in this cast and then we will think about taking if off and getting you into a movable cast and starting therapy. This will be shortly after the first of the year. I wouldn't want to take it off just before Christmas anyway. I've seen too many people strain themselves over a big holiday after surgery or removal of a cast. So sometime after the first of the year we will, at long last, remove this cast. I know you will be glad to get rid of it."

Christmas arrived much too soon. Carl had always enjoyed shopping with Sue for the boys' gifts and picking out something for the granddaughters. He especially enjoyed shopping for Sue. He loved to surprise her and see her beautiful smile. Surprising her with something she loved was something he took pride in every year.

This year Sue would do all the shopping for the family. She was especially busy, but she enjoyed every minute of it, and Carl did help her wrap the presents so he could see what she had chosen for everyone.

He also sat at the table and helped her with her

Christmas baking. She made all sorts of cookies every year. Some were the old family favorites, while others were something new. Sue tried a couple new recipes every year, hoping to find one that the family would want to make a new family tradition. This year the new recipe was one from Katie's mom. Her delicious fruit bar cookies, that she had brought to the workday when Carl was hurt, had been a big hit. Sue had heard how good they were from the boys.

Carl was worried about how he would do his Christmas shopping for a gift for Sue this year. She had been so good to take care of him and he really wanted to have something nice under the tree for her, but had no idea how he was going to manage to sneak something in without her knowing about it.

One day, while Sue was out shopping, Anna stopped in. Carl said, "Anna, I know you are so busy with the girls and Christmas and all you are trying to do, but I really need a favor."

"What is it, Carl? You know I'd be glad to do anything for you. What do you need? Are you thirsty or can I fix you something to eat?"

"No, nothing like that. I need help with some shopping. Sue has to do all of it for everyone in the family. She has done so much for me already, I want something nice under the tree for her. I had thought that maybe she would like one of those big tricycles, she has commented on them a couple times. I saw in the paper where the place on Ninth Street has a sale on them. Do you think you would be able to pick out one? Here is a picture, be sure you get one with a basket and a comfortable seat. You may need Mark to help you out there. I want her to have some jewelry too. She loves opals and, oh, don't forget to get some sort of sewing type stuff. You know how she loves all that. And maybe an outfit, something to wear to church. You be the judge."

Carl was talking faster and faster and getting more and more excited as his list kept growing. "Do you think Katie would help you out, and you two would be able to pick out some really nice things? I'll buy lunch if you girls could help me out."

He took a breath and realized what all he had been asking. He grinned at Anna saying, "Oops, guess I was getting a little carried away. I am asking quite a bit."

"Oh, Carl, go shopping? I don't know. You are right, that would really be asking a lot. It would probably take all day. That would mean a whole day away from the farm and someone would probably have to keep the girls while I went out and had fun. Let's see. If I understand what you are asking here. You want Katie and me to go shopping and spend your money and have lunch on you? That is a lot to ask, but I think Katie and I could probably fit that in," she said with a big grin.

"You look like I'm really imposing on you," he chuckled. Carl pulled out his billfold and gave Anna some money. "Pick out several things for Sue. I know you and Katie will shop wisely and whatever you pick out will be great, I'm sure. If you find something you think she really has to have and need some more money, I could probably scrape up a little more. I've had this stashed away for an emergency, so Sue won't notice it missing out of the checking account or anything."

Anna couldn't wait to tell Katie about the shopping plans. Katie laughed when she heard what they were going to do. "What fun, spending someone else's money!"

Anna's mom was delighted to keep the girls, and plans were made for the upcoming shopping day. They had such a good time and were very pleased with their purchases. The packages were kept at Katie's house and neither girl could wait to see Sue's face when she opened the surprises.

It snowed Christmas Eve, and Christmas morning was a wonderland, truly a gift from God.

Sue was so surprised to find presents from Carl under the tree for her on Christmas morning, when they gathered to open gifts. The first box she opened was jewelry, a beautiful, sparkling pair of opal earrings and matching necklace. Anna said, "I didn't know there was anything to picking out opals, I just found a style I liked and asked Katie if she liked it too. Luckily, Katie knew what to look for; I would have taken the first thing they showed us. However, Katie made them get out about eight pair of earrings and maybe a dozen necklaces of the same style to see which one had the most color and sparkle. These were by far the most beautiful pair in the store, and you have Katie to thank for choosing them. I think they are gorgeous."

Sue thought the earrings were wonderful, and put them in immediately. She put the necklace around her neck and Carl helped her with the clasp. Thinking that was all the presents from Carl, she thanked him and gave him a big hug and kiss. The family went on to other gifts. Sue kept reaching up to touch the gorgeous opals and was overjoyed with the gift.

Soon another gift from Carl was handed to her and she was delighted with the girls' choice of material and sewing supplies. Katie said, "I thought I heard you say something about making a blue and yellow quilt some day, so we picked out several pieces. Anna knew more what you would like in this area. She knew the brands of fabric you liked working with, and after she showed me I could feel the difference. Luckily, I had cut the coupon from the paper the night before, just in case we found something."

When she opened the beautiful navy sweater and skirt, she was elated. "Notice it has a v-neck. They told me that is to show off the opal necklace," Carl beamed.

After opening the last present, Sue got up and started for the kitchen to finish meal preparations. Jodi said, "What about the big one in the garage, Grandpa?"

"Well, I think we better bring it in, don't you?" Carl said.

Mark and Nick went out to get it and Carl told Sue she had to sit down and close her eyes. They brought it in the double French doors to the dining room. Sue could hear the little girls giggling and could hardly stand the wait. Finally, Carl said, "Okay, you can open your eyes."

Sue just squealed, "This is just too much. I love it! Now when you start walking, I can sit in my comfy seat and ride along beside you. Bright yellow, my favorite color, I didn't know they made them in this color! Now, how did you all manage this? I just love it."

"Mark and Nick helped to get it home and they put a big ribbon on the basket. We picked yellow so everyone could see you, and we hope stay out of your way. When you have time to listen I think they have quite a story to tell you about getting it home and hidden. They didn't want everyone in town to see it. Someone might let it slip," Carl said.

"We all had a good time helping Carl shop this year," Anna said.

"I can't wait to get the tricycle out and try it out. When it gets warmer, do you girls want to go for a ride?" she asked Cassie and Jodi.

Of course, they were thrilled; they received new bicycles from Santa and were anxious to go for a spin, as soon as the snow melted. They couldn't wait to take a ride with grandma.

"Are you sure I don't owe you more money?" Carl whispered later.

"No, actually, we owe you thirty-five cents," Anna said, "and we had a wonderful day. We found some sales and Katie had a coupon from the Cotton Patch, so we really had some good deals from everyplace. We had a blast, and lunch, by the way, was delicious!"

"Well, I can't thank you enough. You all did a wonderful job and I appreciate it so much. I think we will all remember this Christmas for a long time," Carl said.

Sue was thrilled with all the wonderful gifts the girls had chosen. Carl said he thought he would just let them do his shopping every year. They had done such a good job. He was pleased with everything they purchased.

Chapter 19

About the only place Carl tried to go with his walker was to church and the doctor's office. He was looking forward to the doctor's visit in January. The only thing on Carl's mind lately was getting this cast removed. The closer it got to the day of the appointment, the more he wanted it off.

Finally, the day arrived. Mark thought this might be a doctor's visit that he should be involved in, so he was at his folks' that morning, and offered to take them.

"There is no need in that, son. We will be fine," his dad said.

"That's okay, I don't have anything else to do. I'll just go along," Mark said as he winked at his mom.

It took quite some time to get the cast off Carl's leg, they really worked him over and he was exhausted by the time it was completely removed.. The nurse had given him a sedative that made him a little sleepy but didn't quite put him out. When the doctor helped him up, he was surprised at how much different it was without the weight of the cast. It really affected his balance.

After removing the cast, the Doctor put a brace on his leg to protect it and give some stability.

He was glad Mark was there to help him make his way from the wheelchair the office provided into the car for his trip home.

The receptionist had set up some appointments and given Sue the information. He was to come back to the doctor in two weeks, and start therapy in three days at the clinic.

On the way home Carl said, "I know they told me not to scratch my leg, but you cannot imagine how this itches. I can't keep my hands off of my leg, the itching is unbearable."

He was determined to regain the use of his leg, so he really tried to do as the doctors and therapist told him to do. One of the therapists was so kind and caring, and tried so hard to help him.

Michelle worked with him two, sometimes three days a week, and bragged on him when he could bend his leg a little farther each time. She told him his determination reminded her of her grandpa. He, too, had been in an accident causing a lot of damage to his leg.

During each visit Michelle shared a story with him about her two little children. Before therapy was over, he felt he knew Michelle's family personally. Of course, he enjoyed telling her about his little granddaughters. Little did he know Michelle, although she did thoroughly enjoy telling stories of her kids, did this to help him relax and ease his mind off the strain of the therapy.

Michelle told him if he went home and sat down, that is how he would spend his life. If he got out and walked regularly, he would get stronger every day.

The doctors and therapist both told him to start out walking to the mailbox and do a little more each day. "You aren't training for the New York marathon; you are only building your strength," Michelle told him one day.

Spring was fast approaching and he knew how he felt every spring, it was a time for a new beginning and he was always eager to start farming. This year he knew he would just have to watch the boys do it all. He couldn't possibly climb in the tractors with his stiff leg.

In the back of Carl's mind, he was concerned as to how he would ever be able to help the boys on the farm. His leg was just not strong enough to make the big step to climb in the machinery. Deep down, Carl wondered if he would ever be that strong, but he kept walking and exercising every day.

The doctors were proud of his progress and with each checkup he got encouragement and praise for working so hard at getting stronger.

One spring Saturday morning, Nick was home from college and Mark was visiting, Carl looked out his favorite window and the boys had three tractors lined up. Carl was wondering just exactly what the boys were up to. He knew he couldn't possibly help them and they were getting everything out to start work today. Katie and her dad pulled in as Carl sat watching what was going on.

Sue was getting their jackets and she said, "If I were you I'd come out and see what these boys and your future daughter-in-law have cooked up."

Carl was able to get around to some extent with a cane now. It was cool out this morning and he could tell the cooler it was, the stiffer his leg was, but he wanted to see what everyone was up to.

Katie's dad was getting something big out of the back of the truck. It was a couple of steps, built perfectly the right size to step up into Carl's favorite tractor. They were made out of lightweight wood so they would be easy for anyone to handle but still very sturdy. Nick had a radio to give his dad.

Mark said "Now, look, Dad, it is like you used to tell us. If you think we are going to do all this work without you, you are mistaken. Get up in that tractor and get busy. We know you can't get in and out of the tractor, so if you have trouble just use this radio and holler at me and I'll come help you out. We will be in the same field most of the time anyway, so all you have to do is use this radio and I'll be right there. We will have this step in the pickup and it is always close by."

Carl thought he was hiding it but everyone could see the big smile as he used the steps to climb up in the tractor, mumbling something about how those boys of his made him work when he wasn't able. Everyone could tell he was thrilled to be out in the field working with the boys doing something useful, something he loved doing.

Chapter 20

Everyone ate at Carl and Sue's that night for supper and Carl was so excited. It was spring and he loved working the ground, getting it ready for planting. "I'll be honest with you all, I thought about the planting season while I was down with this leg during the past winter. Every time I thought about the planting season, I felt sad because I didn't think I would be a part of it. I can't thank you all enough."

Sue said, "I believe that this is the best medicine we have had since he broke his leg. I wish now I hadn't taken such good care of him, and made him get up and work, he seemed to like it so well."

Carl was exhausted, but he had enjoyed the day. Being out with the boys and feeling that he had put in a good day's work made him feel useful. This was the first time he had felt useful since he had taken the terrible fall.

Nick said, "You should thank Katie's dad. He was the one who came up with the idea, and he had even thought to build them out of a lightweight wood so that moving them would not be a problem, even for the girls."

Anna was there for supper, too. She was getting so big

with the baby and felt so miserable, Katie felt sorry for her. It really wouldn't be long now.

Katie and Sue insisted that Anna just sit and visit while they cleaned up the dishes. Of course Cassie & Jodi wanted to help, too. Anna sat and watched, saying her back was hurting and she knew the baby would be here soon. She was already four days late. The doctor told her if she didn't go into labor in a couple more days he would put her in the hospital and induce labor.

At last the dishes were done. The day had been discussed play-by-play at least three times and the following day planned. It was time for everyone to go home. When Anna stood up to leave, a puddle of water seemed to accumulate at her feet. Everyone knew what that meant. Mark helped her to the car and they were soon on their way to the hospital.

Katie asked the girls if they would like to go home with her and have a sleepover. They remembered that she had moved from the wonderful house where they had built the snowman, but it had been awhile since they had been out to her house.

On the way home, even the girls talked about how they liked the house that had once been Katie's grandpa's. They said, "We wish we were staying there."

Katie tried to tell them that the house was going downhill and needed cleaned up and some repairs. The old home place didn't look as it once did or even like it did when Katie lived there.

It made Katie sad to think of the house. She tried not to dwell on it, but to see it succumb to ruins was so depressing. Katie had taken such good care of the house and it held so many memories.

Katie changed the subject before she started to cry, and asked the girls if they were hoping for a little sister or brother. By the time they all discussed the pros and cons of having either a brother or sister, they were pulling in the driveway at Katie's house.

The girls loved Katie and always had a good time when they were with her. They were looking forward to her being their aunt. She played with them and read books and sometimes painted their fingernails and toenails, which was a treat.

They were going to church with Katie in the morning and then on out to the farm. Before Katie turned out the light, Cassie asked, "Katie, do you think our daddy will call before we get up and tell us if we have a baby brother or sister?"

"I bet he will, and I promise when he calls I will let you talk to him even if it is in the middle of the night," Katie told them. She tucked them in and gave each one a hug and kiss.

The alarm went off Sunday morning and Katie's first thought was that they hadn't had a call from Mark. She was worried that something might be wrong. How could she tell the girls if something was amiss? She said a quick prayer, asking God to be with Anna, the baby, and the doctor. The girls would be up soon and asking about the new baby and their mother.

She quietly called Nick to see if they had heard from Mark. He told her that his mother had also been worried, and had run up to the hospital. Anna was having a hard time, the baby was turned the wrong way. They were trying to let it turn on its own, but the doctor was talking about doing a C-section if Anna couldn't deliver soon. It had been a long night for Anna and she was weak, but so far she and the baby seemed to be okay. The doctor did not want this to go on much longer.

Katie thought that maybe she could put off telling the

girls for a little while. She got them up and made a fun breakfast for them. Of course, they started asking about their mom during breakfast. Katie was hoping Mark would call before they left for church.

Just as they were all ready to walk out the door, the phone rang. Katie, once again, said a quick prayer that it would be Mark with some sort of good news. She answered the phone a little hesitantly, and heard Mark's voice on the other end.

She could tell he had been crying. "We have a beautiful baby daughter to go with our other two girls. She is in an incubator right now but she is going to be all right the doctor said," Mark told her.

Katie could tell he was trying to get his voice to a smoother tone before talking to the girls.

"Anna and the baby are both in a weakened condition. We've had a rough night, but we are doing better now. I promised the girls that they could come up and see their mother and the baby, but I don't think that is a good idea for today. Anna is so tired and doesn't look like herself. I'm afraid it would worry the girls."

She let him talk to the girls and they were excited that they had a new baby sister. They had a hard time dealing with not going to see their mother and the baby.

"Girls, the nurses think it would be better for the baby and your mom too, because she needs to rest, if you waited till tomorrow when you get home from school to come up and visit. Besides, you couldn't hold her today, and maybe tomorrow you can. They are going to keep them an extra day, and then on Tuesday they will be at home when you get home from school. And remember, girls, mommy and I love you both," Mark said.

The girls were nearly in tears on the way to church because they couldn't go see the new baby and their mom, but Katie said, "Girls, we have so much to do! After church let's stop by and do some shopping for your baby sister and pick out something really sweet with lots of ruffles for her. What do you think?"

"I don't like ruffles. They always bother me," Cassie said.

Jodi said, "But let's get something pink. Okay?"

"Pink it is, I agree," Katie said. "We will have time to go by and pick something up on the way to the farm, then we can wrap it this afternoon after dinner, and take it in tomorrow when you go see your mom, how will that be? And you both can make special cards for her, too."

"I like that idea," Cassie said.

After church, everyone was at the farm for dinner. Nick and his dad were discussing what they were going to do this afternoon. Taking into consideration that they were short a farm hand due to Mark being at the hospital, and without Anna's help, they wanted to get as much done as possible.

Katie spoke up and said, "Why can't you teach me how to disk? I think I could do that."

Nick and his dad looked at each other, and Carl smiled and said, "Well, she has done everything else out here that she has tried, and always been good help. Let's put her to work! Nick, ride with her for a few rounds, and then, Katie, you be careful. Above all we don't want anything to happen to you."

So that was the start of Katie's official farming career. It seemed from then on she was out helping when she could. The next day, once again because of a calamity in Nick's family, Katie called work, asked for a couple vacation days, and helped on the farm. She enjoyed the work even though it was tiring.

Nick had to go back to school and Mark, of course was

going back to the hospital on Monday. Katie, Sue, and Carl worked in the field together. The steps were in the pickup, so if Carl needed to get out and stretch his leg, go the bathroom or have lunch, Katie and Sue were able to put them up to the tractor. Sue packed lunch and they had a picnic at noon. Carl was glad to be able to walk around, stretch his legs, and eat lunch with Sue and Katie .

"This was such a good idea your dad had, to build these steps and make them light enough that you ladies could help me," Carl said. "I really hope to think of something really nice to do for him sometime."

Carl had started planting beans so Sue stayed around to help load the planter. They were doing good Carl thought, and he told both Sue and Katie he was proud of his new farm hands.

By Monday night, Mark said Anna and the baby were doing so much better. The whole family went up to see them. She was a beautiful baby, and they named her Hannah. Anna was so glad to see the girls. They were so excited to see their mom and meet Hannah, and couldn't wait to take her home. Anna told them how she would need them to help take care of her and the baby when they came home the following day.

The girls didn't want to go to school the next day, but they were assured that when they got home from school their mother and their baby sister would be there waiting for them.

Chapter 21

Nick had one more week and he would have this semester out of the way. He needed to study for exams so it would be a strenuous week, but he was an excellent student and worked hard at school and he felt confident about the upcoming exams.

His interest in the horse operation at the college had grown and he loved spending time with all the horses. The head of the department, Mr. Foutch, had talked with Nick a few times.

One day Nick met Mr. Foutch in the hall. "Nick, I want to encourage you to direct as many classes as you can toward the field of horses. You have a natural talent for working with the horses. Several of the faculty members and the vet have been talking about you. They have seen you in action. I was watching you, myself, the other day from the observation windows in the arena, and I can tell you I was impressed.

I've also been told that you are interested in starting some sort of horse operation of your own, and that is the reason I would like to encourage you to take all the classes you can in that direction. Of course, if you are going to be an Ag. teacher, you have to meet those requirements, too, but every time your schedule allows, I hope you will pick up any and all horse-related classes that you can. I have several booklets and pamphlets filled with information that I'm sure you would find helpful and interesting. I'll put some things together and leave it with my secretary with your name on it. Stop by and pick it up next week."

"Thank you. Thank you very much," Nick said.

Nick was proud of the duties he had earned and eager to prove that he deserved this job. He really enjoyed his work and took the responsibility very seriously.

When he told Katie about his opportunity, he was so excited, and he told her that any extra money he could make, working in the horse barns, he would save toward a house for them when they got married.

He was learning so much, not only from the classes he was taking, but also from being around the barns. The vet was there checking some of the horses at least a couple times a week and Nick would learn something from him nearly every time he stopped in. The vet liked working with Nick. He tried to give him all the tips and encouragement he possibly could in the limited time they had together.

Nick had never dreamed of actually getting into the horse business, before attending MTSU. He had always enjoyed the horses, but enjoyment and recreation were how he considered them. He had never actually considered making a career out of working with something he really loved.

The more he learned, the more he realized that it might be something he could do on the side, as well as working on the farm. As a teenager, he had already done some breaking and training, but there was so much more he could do and learn. He spent more and more time at the barns and everyone who needed help for an upcoming event always requested Nick.

Once the word got out about how good he was with horses, he was soon busy every spare minute. The vet was so patient, and Nick was so excited to learn about the medical care of these animals. Not only the vet, but also the trainers and owners had a lot of information to offer, and Nick was eager to learn.

The warm-up area, directly behind the entrance to the arena, had been strategically placed for viewing from above with the comfort of the owners in mind. Nick thought this was his favorite place to be just before an event, especially a show event. Nick loved working in that area. You could feel the power of the horses ready to surge. The owners and horses alike were keyed up, and the horses could tell that something extra was to be expected of them. Groomed and prepped, the horses pranced with exhilarating anticipation.

Scheduled to stay over several weekends during the summer, Nick was always eager to help with the activities held in the coliseum. It took many people to work the horse shows, rodeos and different activities that utilized the arena there at the school. Everyone who was good with horses was always in demand.

Nick's bank account started increasing little by little, and he started thinking about a house in which he and Katie could begin their lives together. He really wanted to start his life with Katie in a nice house and be able to support her and make her happy. He loved her so much.

During one of his rare weekends at home, Nick had talked with the agriculture teacher at the high school where he had graduated. Mr. Wassermann was going to teach one more year and then retire. Nick wanted to apply for this position.

He knew that a teaching job at his hometown school would be a good opportunity for him. Being close to home and the fact that he would be off during the summer, both definitely had advantages.

He also wanted to get his horse operation underway. The more he thought about this horse operation, the more he wanted to build a barn and start his own business. He wanted a barn with several stalls, in order to be able to board several horses, along with room for the ones he would be breaking and exercising each day.

The stalls at the college were unique to Nick, he wanted to fashion his stalls after that design. There was no way a horse was allowed to start cribbing, or chewing on the wood, in one of those type stalls.

Tossing and turning, he lay awake all night thinking about how much money he could save between now and a year from now, if Katie would be willing to wait another year on him to finish school.

The farm had made his folks a wonderful living through the years, but Nick knew that it wouldn't be enough to support three families: his folks, his brother's family and he and Katie. Mark had already started raising cattle and his operation was working out nicely. Nick had helped him sometimes and he knew if he started some sort of horse operation, Mark would be more than happy to reciprocate. They would work back and forth to help each other. After all, they were family, and that is how their family worked.

He had to try to get some sleep, exams were going to start in a few hours; but Nick felt a little better now that he knew what he wanted to do. He was going to talk to his dad when he got home this weekend to see what he thought. He always respected his dad's advice. Nick had gone through a year or two of thinking he knew more than his dad did, but he finally figured out that sometimes, more often than not, his dad was right. He couldn't understand why some of these kids today were so rebellious and would not listen to a thing their parents told them. He had learned early on that life was easier if you listened to your parents, and they were a lot more willing to help you out if you respected them both.

He chuckled quietly to himself before he fell asleep. Now that he had decided how he was going to support Katie, he just had to see if she would wait that long for him to be able to do all the things that he had planned for her. He figured it would take several more sleepless nights and countless hours of tossing and turning to come up with a plan for where they would live. He had some ideas and he hoped they would all work out in the end. If he could carry out his plan, he thought Katie would be the happiest bride this town had ever seen.

It was so good to finish up with exams at the end of the week, and to go home. School would be out for three weeks before he had to return for the summer courses he had signed up for and to work at the arena.

He was looking forward to helping finish up the planting, and spending some time with family and Katie without having to crack the books.

Chapter 22

Katie was at the house lending a hand, as usual. When Nick arrived home, he, as always, was so glad to see her. At supper, it was just Nick, his folks and Katie, so he broached the subject about his idea for a horse operation, trying for the teaching position, and helping on the farm.

His dad very calmly said, "Well, son, you inherited some of that talent for working with horses from my dad. It passed by me, I never had the patience, but my dad always had a real knack for that sort of thing. He handled the horses in such a calm soothing way, and you handle yourself as he did. I'm glad to see that you are putting your talent to such good use." Carl shook his head slowly back and forth and tapped his fingers on the table, a habit he has had for years. Whenever he tapped his fingers, Nick and Mark always knew he was deep in thought.

Finally he started speaking again. "I know you are a lot younger than I am, and your leg doesn't hurt like mine does, but, son, I'm afraid you are biting off a lot here, maybe more than you can chew. You are talking about three full-time jobs here. Plus, you are getting ready to be married and that alone is a full-time job, just keeping a new bride happy." Katie and Sue both opened their mouths to protest at that remark, but they noticed the big grin on Carl's face about that time. They knew he was just trying to get their attention, and that he did. "I just wondered if you girls were paying attention," he said.

Sue reminded Carl how when they first started out they felt like they could tackle the world as long as they had each other and their faith in God. "We would not be where we are today had we not taken a few chances and gone in over our heads a few times. There were many times we worked till midnight! What am I saying? We still have to work till midnight sometimes and get up early and do it all over again. We have always worked hard and sometimes things didn't work out exactly like we planned, but we were together and I think our love and faith in God kept growing."

Carl drummed his fingers on the table for a few more moments. "This hurts me to say this but, Sue, you're right." A few more minutes of silence followed, then he looked at his wife. "Sue, remember those few acres this side of the creek, that were never suitable for farming? We always hunted mushrooms there. I always thought that would be a good place for something. I just never could decide exactly how I wanted to use that particular piece of ground to its best advantage. Maybe it would be a good spot to build a barn for horses. What do you think, Sue? Better yet, what do you guys think?" He looked over in Nick and Katie's direction.

Sue knew he was asking her opinion about helping Nick and Katie get set up in business and start their lives together. She felt in her heart that it was the right thing to do. With tears glistening in her eyes, all she could do was smile and nod, giving Carl her silent approval. She was so proud of her husband at that moment; she couldn't find the words to express herself.

Carl looked first to Nick and then to Katie. "You may not know where I mean Katie, but, son, you know the place I mean, don't you?"

"Do you have in mind that grove of oak trees on Aunt Annie's old place?"

"That's the one. It would be expensive to clear that piece and make it farmable, but I think we could set up a track around some of those trees. You could train some of your horses there. We probably need to cut a few of the trees.

Some were hit by lightning, and we wouldn't want any left standing that might fall on your buildings, or on someone. I thought about building a barn on that knoll one time years ago, but never got around to it.

Things changed and we didn't have the need these last few years. Those trees around the barn would help keep it a little cooler. It wouldn't flood up there either. That place is on higher ground but looks down on the creek. It seems like a perfect place. What do you think?

We could start working back there as soon as harvest is over. It would take several loads of gravel to make a decent drive back there. I bet Mr. Martin down the road that owns the semi would haul you a few loads at a good price. The location would still be close to home here, so you could help Mark or me out when we needed you and, of course, we might help you out once in a while, if we had to," Carl said, and smiled. Carl was talking slowly and tapping his fingers on the table. It was evident that he was thinking this through as he was speaking out loud.

"Son, with my leg the way it is I know I'm going to have to slow down some and turn more over to you and Mark. We all knew you and Mark would be farming this land eventually, and we certainly want to keep it in the family as long as possible. If you get that teaching job in town, it is only a short drive, plus you would have summers off, and it would be a sure paycheck along with insurance.

We know that it will take a few years before this horse operation brings in a profit, as with any business you would start. It took Mark a while to start turning a profit. He and Anna have both worked hard and I know you have helped him a lot. I look for him to return the favor when he hears about what you want to do. Well, say something. You haven't said much. What do you think?"

Nick was stunned. He hadn't thought of that place down by the creek, which would be an ideal site. He couldn't believe that his folks were offering to help him out that much. He looked at Katie, not sure how she was handling the chain of events. After all, he had not discussed his plans with her earlier. He was thinking now maybe he should have, but he didn't have an opportunity and he didn't expect things to fall into place quite so fast. She was beaming, and huge tears were trickling down her cheeks.

Later Nick couldn't remember exactly what he had said to his dad, but he knew he stammered and stuttered something about working night and day to make it work and paying him back.

"I expect you to! We'll do for you as we did for Mark. You have one year to get going after you get your first horses in the barn. After one year, you have to start making payments on the ground."

"That sounds more than fair to me," Nick said.

With family support and God's strength, anything is possible. Finally, Nick was able to get his emotions in control and speak without breaking up. "I just don't know what to say. I have been thinking and worrying about this and couldn't get it all straight in my mind how and where this would take place. I just never dreamed of anything like this, but I knew if I talked to you we could come up with some sort of solution. I never in my wildest imagination thought of staying on the home place. It is going to be awesome and you'll see, just wait; I'm going to make this work."

"No, we are going to make it work," Katie said. She was like Sue had been earlier, she could barely speak but she managed to smile and nod. Nick put his arm around her and pulled her close.

Finally, Sue cleared her throat, wiped away her tears, handed Katie a Kleenex, and announced, "This calls for a fresh pot of coffee and some of my homemade cookies." This brought everyone back to reality. Nick and Carl decided to go look at the land the next day and see what they needed to get started on this project.

"Dad, just think of it as an investment for you, because if I can get this going, you will not only have me to help on the farm, you get Katie too."

Nick looked at Katie. He wondered if she had thought about how long it would take to get going. "I thought maybe we could get married next April. I know it would be a month before I graduate but the spring farming season would be easier on everyone if we were already married. We wouldn't have time to be thinking about a wedding during planting season, so I thought maybe we could do it before we start planting. If we wait till April, I could have some money saved and you could have the wedding of your dreams," Nick said.

Before she could open her mouth to agree that April would be a good month and would give them time to save more money, Nick launched into his speech. "Katie, I just love you so much and I want to provide a nice house for us to move into when we get married."

She finally just started laughing. "All right! I agree! You've convinced me!" Actually, she had thought they would probably have to wait to get married until after he graduated, so she was happy to have it moved up a couple months. She thought it would be a long wait until April, but she knew they needed to work toward saving money, they needed to find a house, and she had to plan a wedding.

Nick was looking forward to the next day and looking at the land with his dad. He was going to start small, of course, and watch his business steadily grow; at least he hoped that happened. Working at the college had already put him in contact with many people who owned some valuable horses. This could be very beneficial in helping to get his business off the ground. Nick also knew that if he impressed these people at the college, they possibly would be interested in doing business with him in his own endeavor.

Tomorrow while they were looking around at the ground, he would talk to his dad about a house for them to live in when they were married. He had some ideas, but had no concept of how he could pull off the one idea that kept popping back in his mind. It was his favorite plan, but making it all come together would be a big challenge and it had to be a surprise for Katie.

Nick was sure his dad would have some sort of suggestions for that, too.

Chapter 23

Katie missed Nick more and more each week while he was gone to school. She kept herself busy, but it seemed as though the weeks would drag by but the weekend when Nick was home, would fly by. When he came home, it was becoming harder to ignore her romantic feelings and desires and not let them take over.

It seemed as though the preacher had been speaking directly to her last week during his message on Sunday. He had said sex out of marriage is wrong. No matter what the standards of the world are today, it is wrong. Today's society uses all kinds of excuses, but the bottom line is, the morals of today's young people have gone by the wayside.

Katie had always known that, and had always planned to save herself until the wedding night. However, April seemed a long time to wait when you were so much in love and you knew you were right for each other. Lately her emotions had been soaring, almost out of control. When Nick kissed her good night, she wanted to tell him to spend the night with her. She knew she wanted to save this special time for their wedding night, but she was having trouble sticking to her beliefs.

Katie could tell Nick was struggling to hold back some

of his feelings, too. It took longer and longer each evening to say goodnight. They had discussed waiting until after they were married to make love to each other and had both agreed that they wanted to wait and make their wedding night the most special night of their lives.

They had also discussed having children, and they both agreed they wanted to wait a couple of years at least before having their first child. They wanted time to enjoy each other, be settled into their home and their lives, and hopefully save some more money before they became parents.

It was important to Katie to wait until her wedding night and she knew Nick respected her feelings. She was in hopes that with everything they had to do, time would pass quickly, the months would slip by, and their wedding day would soon be upon them.

After hearing the sermon last week and thinking about it, she made a conscious decision to hold fast to her faith and to wait until they were married before having sex. She knew some of her friends were sexually active and she knew they worried themselves sick sometimes, thinking that maybe they were pregnant. She didn't want that to happen, and she didn't want that worry. This was something her mother had discussed with her years before she had met Nick, and she remembered her mother saying how wonderful her wedding night would be if she waited. She did not want to compromise her belief now. She had given it a lot of thought and now she needed to pray about it.

Nick was trying his best to respect Katie's wishes, however, the feelings and sensations running through his body when he was with her sometimes made him wish Katie were not as dedicated to her faith. On the other hand, he knew this would change her completely and she would not be the wonderful girl he had originally fell in love with on that snowy Sunday afternoon when he and his nieces had helped build a snowman. He knew when he held her for that brief kiss afterwards, while the girls waited in the truck, that he was going to marry this girl.

Saturday night, as they were watching a movie at Katie's house, the love scenes became very suggestive and led to some very heavy making out, both on the movie and on Katie's couch. Nick had cautiously slipped his hand up her blouse and had unhooked her bra, as they were gradually slipping down on the couch to almost a complete laying position.

"Nick, we better stop," Katie had said. "Nick," but her words were lost as he covered her mouth with yet another kiss. He did not want to stop.

"We can't stop now. Please, Katie, don't make me stop. Not now, Katie. I love you," Nick pleaded, as he continues to kiss her neck.

"I know, Nick, I love you, too, but I want this to happen in our wedding bed. This is not how I wanted things to happen. Please, Nick, we have to get up. Besides, Nick, what if I were to get pregnant? Neither of us want that to happen. We have to stop."

Things were happening faster and going farther than Katie had intended to allow. At this point, she could see how her friends had gotten into some of their situations. She did not want to tear herself away from Nick's arms at this point either.

Nick held her even closer and gently caressed her body. She held him, too, and they continued to kiss as the couple in the movie was doing, but neither Nick nor Katie was watching the movie at this point. They had long ago lost interest in the couple in the movie, and were only interested in each other. Nick thought that this time he had convinced her to go ahead. This was farther than they had ever dared to go before.

"No, Nick, I'm not going to let this happen, we are going to stop now." This time, as she was speaking, she was squirming away; she did not continue to kiss him.

"Katie, I love you, but I know you are right. I think that maybe I should go home for the evening," Nick said. "If I stay it is only going to be hard on both of us."

After that evening, they tried to be more careful and not get quite so carried away. Both of them agreed that the next time they did not think they would be able to stop.

Chapter 24

K atie started making a mental list of all the things she needed to do to plan their wedding. Shop for a dress, meet with the florist, reserve the date for the church, and talk to the preacher, just to mention a few. Things were coming to mind so quickly, she started taking notes. She was hoping the addition to the church would be complete and they could be married in the new sanctuary.

The schedule for completion for the new three-million-dollar sanctuary and addition to the church was the last of March. It was going to be one of the most spectacular churches in southern Illinois. The board was hoping to hold the first service in the new sanctuary on the first Sunday of April. In addition, Katie was hoping to have the first wedding in the new building. Everyone in the congregation was excited about the new building and construction was moving along on schedule.

Katie had visualized it many times in her head. Spring flowers would adorn the church, and the bridesmaids would be dressed in a beautiful shade of purple that would match the iris that bloomed on the west side of her parents' home every spring. She needed to make a note to tell her dad to redo the bulbs this fall and fertilize them so there would be dozens of beautiful blooms for her wedding. He loved sharing his beautiful iris and always took bouquets to several of the neighbors. She thought using them for her wedding would make him proud. He really had raised some prize flowers. He had entered them in the fair one year, took first place and went on to state, taking first place there also. There were other colors, too, but she had always been partial to the purple ones. Other spring flowers would be in bloom, too. She was hoping to use daffodils, lilacs and hyacinths in addition to the iris blossoms. The hyacinths and lilacs both had such a distinct fragrance and they were all her favorites.

One of the board members had shown her the architect's plans that showed what the church would look like when it was finished inside. She could envision herself standing at the altar beside Nick with her long train draping the steps that went up to the platform in the front of the church.

She could not wait to go shopping for her wedding gown. Trying on some of the wedding dresses she had seen in the windows seemed like a dream. Katie was anxious to put herself in that dream, but still afraid someone would wake her up.

She had been so very busy she hadn't actually had time to go and try on wedding gowns. The one magazine issue of bridal gowns that she broke down and purchased was wearing thin, she had thumbed through the pages so many times. There were some gorgeous gowns in there. She was in hopes of finding something beautiful, elegant and flowing, but not outrageously priced. Ruffles and bows were not her thing, but she did want an elegant train.

One of her best childhood friends Cheryl would be maid of honor and Anna would be a bridesmaid, that was for certain. Of course, Cassie and Jodi would be in the wedding and Nick would have to pick who he wanted for his groomsmen. She knew Mark would be his best man, and Nick needed to make a decision as to the other groomsman as well.

He also needed to be thinking about a house for them to live in, but lately he seemed to have his mind on other things. She was beginning to get a little annoyed that he wouldn't even talk about a place for them to live.

He would talk about the wedding. In fact, it seemed as though he enjoyed helping to plan the event. He had shown her the kind of tux he preferred in the magazine, and had put in several suggestions about decorations that Katie really liked.

They had already talked about several places to go on their honeymoon. She had tried to talk about the honeymoon with him one evening and then bring in where they were going to live when they got home. It didn't work.

"But Nick, why won't you talk about where we will live? We will need to know where we are going when we get off the plane from the honeymoon!"

He would always hug her and give her a quick kiss, "Come on Katie, get off it. Just be patient. We'll find something. It's early yet. Didn't you listen to the sermon Sunday? In God's time, Katie, that is what the preacher said, and you have to be patient."

"I know, Nick, but I just want some sort of idea. Do you think we'll rent for awhile? Are there any houses in your area that you think might be for sale soon? I can't help it Nick. I just want an image in my mind, I guess so I can dream about it. Will we need lots of furniture? I could be making curtains if I knew where we were going to live, or going to rummage sales and finding some used furniture. I just want an idea, and I can't help it. We could be saving money if we got a house and I moved in it. I could be putting money toward it rather than my old house. Doesn't that sound like a good idea?"

"I don't know right now, Katie. It's too early. I'll think about it. We've got nearly a year... well, almost. Now, just drop it, Katie, please! We will not live on the streets, I promise you."

As those big brown eyes looked up at him in disbelief, he could see tears welling up. He realized he had sounded a bit more harsh than he had intended. "I'm sorry to bother you, Nick," she said.

"Oh now, Katie, I didn't mean to sound so grouchy. I'm sorry. Let's change the subject."

"Sure, that's normal. We always change the subject when I bring up where we will live."

"All right, I promise I will give it more thought. But right now I have to get through school, I have a job, a wonderful girlfriend and I'm trying to help dad on the farm," he said as he took her in his arms, rubbed her back and held her so close.

"Okay, the wonderful girlfriend part was a good remark in your favor. You get points for that, but I can't help it. I love you so much and I can't help thinking about where we will live. I want to have it fixed up so cute for us to live in after the wedding."

Chapter 25

Since she knew Nick was going to be at the school a lot during the summer working with the horses to earn extra money, she decided she, too, would get an extra job. She wanted to be able to contribute equally with Nick, both for the wedding, and for the future. Until she found an extra job she planned to help her dad paint their house. It needed it desperately, and she could get some sun while she was helping him. He had done so much for her; there was no way she could ever fully repay him.

Katie and her dad had taken a break from working on her house until she and Nick decided where they were going to live. She didn't want to put more money into the old place if she was going to be moving soon.

Early one Saturday when Nick's schedule did not allow for a trip home, she started painting at her folks' house, with her dad's help. Overcoming her fear of heights, she climbed the ladder and started to work. At first, she was very slow and kept looking down.

"Don't look down so much, Katie. Pay attention to what you are doing," her dad said several times.

She was making a conscious effort not to look down but it was a struggle. She was a little nervous, being up that high, but she wanted to help her dad and she wanted to do a good job.

"Relax, Katie. Concentrate on what you are doing, and not the ladder," he said.

Before long, Katie was aware that she was more relaxed and was handling herself on the ladder with more control and finesse.

"Hey, Dad, I think I'm getting the hang of this! I may be able to do this after all."

After lunch, Katie was really feeling the effects of going up and down the ladder so many times. Her leg muscles had started to tighten, and her shoulder was beginning to stiffen from moving the paintbrush back and forth. She didn't realize how out of shape she had become, and how tense she had been while standing on the ladder.

As she was climbing back up to her painting position, she heard a familiar sound. It was Nick's little pickup coming down the road. What a wonderful sight.

"I managed to get away a few hours earlier than I expected, so here I am to help paint. Am I too late?" Nick asked.

"Does it look like it? Grab a brush!" Katie was so excited to see him; she could have lept off the ladder. However, she resisted the urge since just hanging on and painting at the same time seemed to be a challenge.

Nick said, "Come on down. I'll paint up there and you start catching up on the lower part."

"You got a deal," Katie said. "You know, by the time we finish this I may need a few appointments with your dad's therapist."

The job progressed much faster with Nick helping them. Late that evening a neighbor stopped by and he commented on how nice it looked. Katie's dad bragged about her work. He said, "Katie is helping me for a change now, but she wants to earn some extra money for her up-coming wedding. She has even conquered her fear of climbing the ladder. She is really doing a good job, and so is Nick."

He was proud of his future son-in-law and felt they were the perfect match, wanting the entire community to know Katie was marrying a good Christian young man. Nick felt a little embarrassed as Katie's dad continued to tell the neighbor what a good job the kids would do on his house if he wanted to hire them.

"Sounds like you got good advertisement," Buzz, the man from down the road, said to Katie . "You can start as soon as you get this house done, if you want to. I'll go to town and get the paint in the morning."

Nick and Katie could see dollar signs, so they got busy finishing up at her folks' house and proceeded to move on to the neighbor's project the following week. He had a two-story house, but Katie was determined to meet the challenge head on.

Word spread that the kids were working to earn money toward a house of their own. Another neighbor, and then a family member stopped by and before they knew it, they had four or five projects lined up to paint. They explained that with Nick working at the horse arena and going to school, and Katie working full time, their time would be limited and it might take a little longer to finish a project.

The people were patient. They totally understood time was a valuable commodity. Katie was getting a reputation as a very conscientious painter and they were willing to wait in order to get a job well done. Besides, they were helping young people in the community, and they all delighted in doing that. Nick tried to help Katie and her dad every time his schedule allowed. The projects, one by one, were completed, some big and some small. Everyone seemed to be pleased with their new paint job.

No sooner would one project get finished, another task would appear. Katie was so busy all summer painting with her dad that she didn't realize how fast the time had flown. Before she realized that the summer could be over, Nick's folks began to discuss plans for the harvest. Katie had worked hard all summer and Nick had worked either with her and her dad, or at the arena when he wasn't in class. They were both exhausted.

When they realized how the bank account had grown, they were quite proud of themselves. Nick couldn't brag on Katie enough, saying she had done so much of the work. He was so proud of her for many reasons, for not only the hard work, but also, the money she had saved would go toward their house. The golden tan she had managed to perfect made her even more beautiful. He knew God had blessed him with a beautiful, hard-working young woman and he was so pleased that she was going to marry him. She had no idea how much he really loved her.

Katie had somehow managed to meet with the florist, and rent a place for the reception, along with making time to go to several of the events at the horse arena at Nick's college during the summer. She still needed to shop for a dress, but she knew she would get that done. She didn't want to get it too early and then gain or lose weight. Actually, she was getting anxious to go shopping for her gown.

Katie was beginning to think that work was all they did. They had worked well together, whether on the farm or their moneymaking projects during the summer, they had both accepted the responsibility and plunged forward. When Katie was able to go to the events at the college, they found they both had a love for horses, and she enjoyed helping him if she could.

There hadn't been much time for relaxation during the summer months, they were both busy every spare minute, but it had been a fun and profitable experience. Katie had enjoyed going to the coliseum on several occasions, and she had learned a lot from just watching Nick.

"Katie, I can't wait to start our lives together. Don't you wonder sometimes how big our horse operation will be and what our first child will be? Sometimes my mind tries to imagine us with a kid. I think I have a lot of growing up to do myself before we have a baby. However, it's fun to day-dream about the future."

"Yes, Nick, I do love to dream about our future together."

If he could read her mind now, he would surely know that all that was on her mind now was their future, the wedding, and a house. If he was daydreaming about them together, where were they living? She knew better than to mention it.

They had talked about the wedding plans but when she brought up the subject of a house, something always happened to change the subject. She even noticed the other night when she mentioned where they would live, Sue changed the subject, and Carl just got up and left the room.

She had mentioned living in the little house she lived in, but Nick had said that would be too far from the farm, and it was too small. Therefore, if they weren't going to live in her house, with the wedding coming up in less than a year, shouldn't they at least be talking about where they *were* going to live?

It had seemed like so long to wait 'till they got married, but as the fall harvest was approaching she knew that the months were slipping by. She knew that harvest would consume everyone's complete attention until all the crops were out of the fields. There would be no talk of a house for a couple months at least.

Katie was beginning to get a little depressed. She didn't share the family's enthusiasm for the start of the new season as she usually did. There would be a lot of work and she would be in the center of all the activities, as always, but she couldn't help think of the old house she had lived in at grandpa's place. There was already a barn there, and enough land to have put a track out back to exercise the horses. Oh, how she had loved that house. It was a house that had character. It welcomed you when you came in and made you feel warm all over, whether you lived there, as she had for a while, or if you were just visiting.

Katie couldn't help but day-dream a little and think about what fun it would have been to raise a family in the old house. It was so roomy and had so many possibilities, as the family grew. The upstairs had so much potential for a cute little girl's room, with the dormer windows. She would have loved to have had a room like that for her very own when she was a little girl. However, if they had a whole house full of boys, that would work too.

She shared a few of her dreams with Nick sometimes. He usually said something like, "Oh Katie. There are plenty of other houses," or "Now, Katie. That's not the only house in the world."

Well, she better just come back to reality and stop daydreaming. After all, she had a wedding to finish getting together, and a job to go to five days a week. She also needed to help with the harvest at Nick's family farm. Nick's family took it for granted that she would be there.

Time did not allow her to daydream about something that would never happen.

Carl had paid her for the work she had done in the spring. He told her with Anna in the hospital, Mark having to be gone to see about her, and Nick in school, they would have had to hire someone else in order to get the crops in. She was such good help they didn't have to bring anyone else in. He paid her every week, and he paid her generously. He knew she would save it for their house. He had already told her that he was going to pay her if she helped in the fall, too.

The temperatures had been perfect to create such beautiful vibrant colors throughout the woods. She just loved admiring the foliage as she made her many trips to the elevator. It was a gorgeous autumn and it was the topic of conversation everywhere she went. Everyone was talking about the autumn colors. It was one of the most breath-taking, colorful fall seasons they had seen in the past decade.

The yellows and oranges lit up the trees. The news media had covered the gorgeous colors and had shown pictures of some of the more outstanding trees in the area on the evening news. The weather was perfect and everyone worked as hard as they could to get the combining done before it started raining.

"Before it starts raining." Everyone in Nick's family was using that phrase. She had never heard the family mention the fall rains so much. Everything they did, they wanted to get it done before the rains. She was wondering if they expected the monsoons to hit any day. The rains seemed to occupy their minds as much as a house occupied hers.

"Dad and I have a lot of work to get done before bad weather sets in. I sure hope we can get everything done," Nick told Katie.

"Let me guess," Katie said, "before it starts raining, right?"

Nick smiled, "You guessed it."

"What are you going to do first?" Katie asked.

"Oh, just stuff, you know. There is just a lot of work to do," Nick said.

"That was pretty vague. I hope you didn't give out too many details," she answered.

Chapter 26

She was determined that the first Saturday after the harvest was complete, she and Nick would start looking for a house. At least, she was going to insist they sit down and talk seriously about it. However, for some reason Nick kept putting off even having a discussion of their living arrangements.

However, her plans were short-lived. Her mother insisted that on that particular day she had to go shopping for a dress for the wedding.

"Mother, I don't even have my dress! And all the stores are going to have in stock are winter dresses."

Nevertheless, Barbara would not take no for an answer, saying, "Katie, there may be a dress on sale somewhere that will be just perfect for a mother-of-the-bride's dress. We never know what kind of weather we will have in April. I may need one with a jacket. Besides, it will be fun. How often do you get to go shopping for your daughter's wedding gown and a dress to wear to your daughter's wedding? I'm excited, Katie, and I can't wait to see you try on some wedding gowns! Aren't you anxious to see how you look as a bride? I've dreamed about this day since you were born."

Katie thought it did sound like fun, and Nick seemed to think he was going to be busy working with his dad, so she decided a short shopping trip would be nice for her and her mother. She figured her mother would just want to go to the neighboring town for a few hours as she always did.

Delaying their house hunting plans, or at least *her* house hunting plans for another few days, would not make that much difference if it would keep everyone else happy.

"Mom, I'll come by and pick you up in the morning and we will go into town," Katie told her mom.

"Oh, no," her mom insisted, "I'll come up to your house and we will go from there. Maybe we can check out several bridal shops while we are in St. Louis. I think that would be exciting, but I don't want you to think we have to buy a gown the first day. We will need a couple of these shopping days. After all, I only have one daughter."

St. Louis, Katie thought, she was shocked that her mother wanted to go that far. She had no idea that her mother would be so excited about her wedding.

Once again, Katie's plans were changed. Instead of a few hours' shopping spree, this would be an all-day event. As for the house hunting plans, they were put on the back burner, and it seemed as though Nick had lucked out again.

"How often do you get to do this sort of thing?" Barbara was so excited about going shopping at a place in St. Louis that someone had apparently told her about. It supposedly had designer gowns at a discounted price.

They left early Saturday morning, enroute to this illusive shop that was supposedly the best bridal shop west of the Mississippi, to hear her mom talk about it.

Katie was surprised at her mom. She just shopped,

looked, tried on things, and seemed to go on and on about some things that Katie would never have thought about her mom even noticing. This was unusual for her mom. She seemed to be having such a wonderful day that Katie didn't have the heart to hurry her along. They had laughed more today than Katie could ever remember.

Possibly, if they got home early enough, Katie and Nick would still be able to talk about a house, but it didn't look like that was going to happen.

Barbara said, "This is such a special day. We need to go to that wonderful Italian place on the hill to eat. It is a little distance from here, but they have excellent food. Your dad took me there for my birthday last year."

It took forever, because they served the meal in courses and it was such a crowded place. "This must be a very popular place," Katie said.

After a two-hour lunch, which proved to be very delicious, and time-consuming, they were ready to proceed on their shopping trip. They had discussed several plans for the wedding and came up with numerous new ideas about the reception, all of which Katie had jotted down on her napkin. All in all, much to Katie's surprise, she had relaxed and enjoyed the lunch with her mother, and felt they had made several decisions about the wedding.

The next stop was the wonderful bridal shop that she had heard so much about, and it had more dresses in Katie's size than she would have thought available in three stores. Katie was overwhelmed. Her mother had not been misled. The friend had not begun to describe how wonderful this shop was, and all the gowns were gorgeous. "How will I ever be able to choose? They are all so beautiful."

Katie tried on several gowns while her mom made some notes about the ones Katie really liked and their prices. Trying on the satin gowns put Katie in an excellent mood. She was excited about the flowing skirts and lengthy trains, and was more than willing to go to another bridal shop, when her mother suggested it, to try on even more dresses.

Katie found one that was exactly like the one in the magazine that she had drooled over. She fell in love with it. Both Katie and Barbara had gasped when she walked out of the dressing room. Katie, seeing herself in the full-length mirror and her mother watching from the viewing area, were both breathless. She felt like a princess in the elegant gown, and her mother had to dab a Kleenex to her eyes as the tears formed and threatened to trickle down her cheeks.

"This is the dress," Katie announced.

Katie's mother suggested she wait a few days to buy it. After all, this was the first day she had looked.

When they got in the car, her mother said, "Katie let's look close to home and see what they have first. If your gown needs altered or anything, it will be easier to go for fittings. If there is nothing close to home that you like as well, we will come back and get this one.

It did look exquisite on you. You dad will be very pleased with your choice, and Nick will burst his buttons when he sees you coming down the aisle. I think it is a good idea to check closer to home before we buy anything."

"I agree, but it was a wonderful day. I felt so elegant in those gowns. It was breathtaking to be able to try on some of them. Thank you, mom, for insisting that we go shopping today. I can't begin to tell you how much today has meant to me. I did have a wonderful day. Some of those gowns were magnificent."

Katie was really beginning to feel a little tired. Between the driving and the long heavy meal, she was ready for a nap. However, her mother seemed to be enjoying the day so much she couldn't bring herself to suggest they head for home. Barbara insisted on buying Katie a few things and she found a chair and relaxed while Katie tried on several casual outfits for work.

Finally, her mom said, "I think that first dress I tried on in the quaint little shop was my favorite and would look really nice for your wedding. It is the perfect dress. If it is a warm day, I can wear it as a sleeveless dress. I could slip on the jacket in case it rained, or if it is a little cool. Katie, did you notice it had the iris color of purple in the skirt?"

"Yes, it did. I didn't think about that. You are right it's a good choice for the wedding. Do you want to go back across town and get it today?"

"I really don't think I will find anything I like that well or that will be as suitable for the occasion as that dress. I know it is a long way to go back there, but let's go back and get it or we may be sorry," her mother said.

There was nothing to do but take her mom back to that store and buy the dress. Now, Katie was sure they would be on their way home.

She couldn't believe her ears when her mom asked her to stop for coffee and maybe dessert at their favorite café on the way home. Katie and her mother had had a wonderful day together and she assumed her mom did not want it to end. "Truthfully," Katie thought, "neither do I. This had been very special, a once-in-a- lifetime day.

Over the years, on the rare occasions when they had gone shopping in St. Louis, it was always an exciting day. As she was growing up, she could remember going across the bridge to go shopping only for special events. They had gone for prom dresses, and one time even for a suit for her dad. A few times they had gone to visit a friend in the hospital. On the way home they always stopped at a favorite quaint little café and bakery, for dessert and coffee. She, as a child, had always had chocolate milk. No trip seemed to be complete unless they stopped at their favorite establishment. Katie loved their homemade bread. It was her favorite. They always took home several loaves, along with special bakery products.

"Mom, do you remember the time I got sick on the chocolate covered donuts we got here? Everything here is so delicious, and I just couldn't get enough of them. I sneaked another one or two after you and dad had said I had enough."

"Yes Katie, I do remember. Your dad said this morning, be sure you stop at the bakery and bring home some bread but don't let Katie have chocolate covered donuts." They both laughed.

When they got home, her mom said, "We would like to take you out for dinner after church tomorrow, and Nick, too, if he is available. We will just plan on coming up to your house, pick you up and take you to church, and then out to eat."

This was again something out of the ordinary for her parents. They normally didn't attend the same church she did. She wondered why her mother had added, *if Nick were available*, that would never have been a problem a few weeks ago. Her mother was right though, sometimes Nick was not available to spend time with her. She agreed and promised to call Nick and find out what he had going for tomorrow. Maybe he would have time to fit her in.

"I'm planning a wedding. I've spent all day shopping with my mother for a wedding gown and a dress for her to wear to my wedding, and I don't know if the future groom will have time to eat Sunday dinner with me. Now, there is a cheerful thought. Okay, mom, we will see." Katie said to her mother.

"Oh, now, honey. Don't get worked up. You know Nick, he is just working on a few things," her mother said. "You should know by now how it is out on the farm, always something to do or fix. Don't worry! We will see you in the morning."

She couldn't believe it. She was totally worn out and her mom was already making plans for tomorrow. Her plans for the evening were to take a nice shower, curl up and work on the neglected quilt that had once been a priority to finish before the wedding day.

Nick called to check on her soon after she got in the house and it was good to talk to him for a while. She told him all about her day. He chuckled and said, "Sounds like your mom did a good job," stopping abruptly "A good job wearing you out." He thought it was hilarious that they had to go back and buy the first dress she had tried on.

He told her he had done some work where they were going to build the small barn to start their little business. Mark and his dad had helped him and they had just gotten in the house. He was tired, but he would see her at church in the morning.

When she mentioned they were asked out to lunch, he told her he would eat lunch with them but needed to get back to the farm and do a few things before returning to college.

She tried to bring house hunting into the conversation, but as always Nick said, "Be patient, Katie. We'll get to it. You just have to give me a little time."

Another weekend gone with nothing even discussed about a house. Well, she would do her part as far as plans for the wedding and leave the house worry to him. It did seem to Katie that he could at least talk about it, but all he was interested in were the horses.

Obviously, no matter how hard she tried, she could not leave the house worry to him. It was going to be such a major part of their life, of course, and she was concerned.

Chapter 27

Katie couldn't control her anxiety about the house. As time went by and the wedding drew closer, she couldn't help but wonder where they would live. If they bought an older house, she knew it might need a fresh coat of paint and windows washed. With Katie's experience with older homes, she figured that would just be minor. It would probably need some major repairs. That did not seem to worry Nick. He did not seem concerned about where they were going to live.

Maybe they would live in the loft of the barn he was going to build for the horses. He seemed to be much more interested in working on that project than looking for a house. Finding a house was near the top of Katie's list of things to do, and it would take some effort on Nick's part.

A hot steamy shower sounded enticing, just what she needed to help her unwind from the day and relax. The hot water beating down on her body seemed to relax some of the knotted muscles, and she continued to stand there taking several deep breaths, as the steam from the shower seemed to clear her head. She had stayed in the shower, letting the water pulsate as she closed her eyes and relaxed, much longer than she realized, when she felt the hot water start to cool. It was definitely time to get out and dry off. Sort of like her love life, she thought, sometimes almost too hot and then turning to a much too cool temperature.

Settling down to do a few stitches on the quilt while she watched the news and weather, seemed to make her feel better, as always. She was a little upset. Well, maybe a little upset was putting it mildly.

Try as she may, she could not understand Nick's disinterest. Was he losing interest in her or just finding a house? As she proceeded to take out her frustrations with the needle, she found the more she worked, the calmer she felt. Her fingers worked diligently and the blocks started going together easier than in the beginning.

Remembering the dresses that grandma had made her out of some of the fabric had a calming effect on Katie. She could almost feel she was once again in the old home place sitting in front of the warm fireplace, stitching on the flower garden pattern that her grandma had started years ago. She was remembering when she started on this quilt, the way she and Nick felt about each other. They could hardly keep their emotions in control, and now she barely saw Nick at all.

Feeling herself beginning to dose, she decided it was time to go to bed, and maybe a good night's sleep would make her feel better.

She accomplished quite a bit on the quilt that night. Before turning in Katie had to spread out the blocks she had been working on and admire what she had accomplished.

Sleeping very soundly, she dreamed most of the night about living in grandpa's house. In the first part of the dream, she could see them so plain. They were walking across the yard of grandpa's house, hand in hand. She was still in her beautiful wedding gown and Nick, looking so very handsome in his tuxedo, had his arm around her, and they were laughing.

They looked so happy, just like when they had first started dating. As they went up the porch steps, Nick holding her arm to help her, he then swung open the front door and swept her off her feet in one swift gesture. He was carrying her over the threshold. When he set her down in the living room, Katie woke up. She wanted to return to the dream, so she tried not to stir. Maybe she could drop back into the sleep that had been so sweet.

In a short time, it happened. She was back in grandpa's house. The dream was so vivid. She was married to Nick and they were fixing up a nursery for their first addition to the family. They seemed so happy. She could see Nick putting the final touches on the wallpaper border, as she sat in the rocking chair looking on. They seemed to be in the back bedroom of grandpa's house. She could see that she was enormously pregnant in the dream.

She then woke with a start! The dream was over. It had been such a sweet dream, but one that Katie knew would never come true in her grandpa's house. She had to smile to herself thinking about how she looked, as she was pregnant in the dream. It was still dark outside, but Katie was wide awake. She drug herself out of bed and made a fresh pot of coffee.

Sunday morning came with a beautiful sunrise. Since Katie was up so early, she took her coffee out on the back step and enjoyed watching the sun climb ever so slowly over the woods just east of her little house. The fall colors seemed to glisten as the rays of sunlight hit the leaves. It was the most breathtaking sunrise Katie could remember. It made her think of her friend, Margaret, from work, who always walked her dog early every morning. She would always comment if there had been an exceptional sunrise, and this morning was definitely one of those mornings.

She relived the dream of the night before and basked in the warm feeling it brought to her, as her heart seemed to skip a beat.

It was beginning to be chilly in these early morning hours, but that was just normal for this time of year. She decided to go in and warm up her coffee. It would soon be time to shower and get ready for church.

They all attended church together, Nick meeting them at the front door. While eating lunch, she mentioned driving out to the farm, thinking her folks would enjoy going out there for a visit. The response was unanimous. Nick and her parents all looked at her with a panicked look and said "No," in unison.

"Okay, we won't go," Katie said.

"Well, I've got a lot to do, and then leave shortly for school," Nick said.

"I've got to get home and do some laundry," her mother stammered.

Her dad faked a yawn, and said, "I was thinking about a long nap."

This Sunday had been a full day and when evening came and her folks had gone home, Katie thought back about her day. It was a little strange, but maybe her folks just wanted to be around her more since she was getting married soon. It felt as though they were guarding her, or at least watching her closely. Guarding seemed like such a strong word.

Such a bizarre feeling came over Katie as she thought about it. It almost felt as though she was being protected from finding out something, maybe something horrible. What if Nick was sick? "Please God, don't let anything be wrong with him. Even if he doesn't love me anymore, don't let him be sick," she said aloud.

She wondered why they had all looked so alarmed when she mentioned going to Nick's house to visit. Nick stumbled around and said the folks were busy today, and her dad said he just did not want to drive out there and bother people on Sunday afternoon. It seemed like they kept making excuses and were trying to cover up something.

Why was everyone changing her plans, even the very small minute details? She just couldn't understand, but she had noticed a change in everyone she was around. Stop worrying about it. This is just something you have brought on yourself. You are just under a lot of stress and it is really nothing, she tried to tell herself.

It had now been several weeks since Katie had been out to the farm. That seemed like a long time, since many times she was out there every day, but no one suggested she come out. Really, she felt like they didn't want her. They usually always called and asked her out for supper at least one night during the week when Nick was gone. They hadn't called her at all, not to ask her out to the farm, or just to say hello. She was beginning to wonder if she was paranoid. First, she thought they were watching or guarding her, and now she felt neglected.

Katie had barely seen Nick lately, and he didn't seem to be making an effort to see her. Maybe he was afraid she would bring up house hunting. She had worked herself up tonight and now felt depressed. She had been so excited yesterday about trying on the gowns, but now it seemed as though he didn't have time to be bothered with her. She always looked forward to seeing Nick, particularly on the weekends and things were strangely different lately.

She would show them all. If they didn't want her to

come out there, she would stay home and work on her quilt. Whether or not it would go on a bed for her and Nick, she wasn't real sure about that anymore. A little self-pity and depression seemed to be overcoming her.

Katie was beginning to wonder if he really wanted to marry her. At that point she began to cry. She couldn't bear the thought of not being married to Nick. She was so in love with him, and had thought he also loved her. The tears streamed down her face and dropped on some of the beautiful quilt blocks. She, for the first time since she had dated Nick, was beginning to have doubts.

Once again, by the time she finally felt sleepy enough to go to bed, she was amazed at how many blocks she had sewn together. It wouldn't be long till she had enough blocks that she could set the top together. She had thought earlier that she would have someone at the church quilt it for her.

Nevertheless, she was beginning to think that maybe she might tackle the quilting herself. She knew it would be a major undertaking, but after all, she had those wooden quilt frames in the attic that her dad made. Lately she seemed to have more time on her hands, since she didn't seem to be dating anyone. Maybe she would be able to quilt it all herself, since she seemed to have more free time lately.

Her birthday was the week of Thanksgiving. She wondered if Nick would even remember, let alone make time for her. He had been preoccupied lately. His mother always said birthdays were so important, and they always got together to celebrate everyone else's birthday. She wondered if his family would have time to get together for her birthday.

She hadn't talked to Anna in quite awhile. Katie really missed talking with Anna and going places with her. She couldn't help wonder if she had done something to offend the whole family, but couldn't imagine what it could have been. The last time Katie had called Anna, she got rather short, curt answers, and all of a sudden, Anna found an excuse to hang up and had never returned the call.

Katie knew the baby had probably grown since she had seen her last. She would have loved to see Anna and all the little girls. She loved all three of the darlings, who she thought would be her nieces one day, and missed them terribly. I wonder if they miss or ask about me, she thought.

When she went to bed that night, as every night, she prayed to God. This time she asked him to help her understand what was going on. She loved Nick and his whole family and wanted things to be as they were before. She needed some guidance to figure out what, if anything, was wrong. If she had done something to upset them, she wished with all her heart they would tell her what exactly she had done. She would apologize.

Her own parents were acting very strangely. They got nervous every time she mentioned coming to their house. She decided they didn't want her to come and visit anymore than Nick's family did.

Chapter 28

Another week passed with the same routine evolving. She went to work and Nick went to college. Nick, occasionally, would find a few spare minutes to give her a call, but most of the time he was just too busy to fit her in. She had given up asking if she could help. There was always some excuse as to why they didn't need her, and she was not going to ask again.

Sometimes her folks met her for lunch, which would prove to be the highlight of her day. After work, she would then go home, same boring routine every day. For her evening meal, sometimes she would eat something light or grab a salad on the way home. She didn't have an appetite at all anymore. She had to force herself to eat. After she choked something down, she would then work on her quilt.

She had wanted to lose a few pounds before the wedding, but now she had no appetite at all, and had already dropped eight pounds. The way she was losing weight at the present, if she had bought the dress, it would be falling off of her by the wedding. She wondered if she would be able to get the dress in a smaller size; then she wondered if she would need the dress at all. Why think about the wedding dress, she thought to herself. Obviously, Nick was not too interested in getting married.

Barbara tried to talk Katie into another shopping day to try on some more wedding dresses, but Katie had stood her ground this time, and refused to go. She just wasn't in the mood to go wedding shopping.

When she got home from work, she had no desire to work on her house. All the projects she had planned of painting or papering had just gone by the wayside. She had thought at first the more she fixed it up the more money it would bring if she sold it, but she now had no energy or enthusiasm, so she would just curl up with her quilt.

If she and Nick did get married they wouldn't live here, and she had now decided that if the wedding didn't go as planned, she was going to move, maybe even to a different city.

Nick was always so busy working that he didn't have much time for her at all and the family was so distant.

If they didn't get married, what would she do? She couldn't imagine not marrying Nick. She didn't even want that thought to cross her mind, but it had, and it made her sick.

Sometimes she thought he was obsessed with this horse operation, both the one at the college and the business he wanted to start at home. That was always his excuse for being busy. He and his dad and brother were working on the barn, or the track, or something, and he didn't seem to want her around.

Then, on occasion, she imagined that maybe there was another girl. She couldn't believe that Nick would be that type of guy. She didn't think he would have someone else on the side, but she was beside herself with worry. Something was going on, she couldn't figure out what it was, but she knew without a doubt that something was different.

In fact, she hadn't been out to her folks' house in a while either. Every time there was a possibility of her going out to their house, they wanted to come to her house or meet her in town.

Chapter 29

April, and the tentatively planned wedding, was less than six months away. If Nick wanted to back out of this wedding, it would be nice if he would at least tell her before she spent any more money. This was on her mind twenty-four hours a day. She couldn't sleep, couldn't eat, had no energy or desire to work on the wedding, and couldn't stop crying when she was alone. She lost another five pounds and was having migraine headaches more and more frequently.

One of the women at work put her arm around her. "Try not to worry, Katie, you have got to pull yourself together, it is just pre wedding jitters. If you lose much more weight, honey, that wedding dress will fall off of you!"

Katie had to smile, as this philosophy seemed to echo her thoughts of only a day or two ago.

Being much easier said than done, Katie thought to herself, she shook her head yes, and wiped away the tears that were forming in her eyes. The days of wearing mascara were over a few weeks back.

"I haven't bought one yet, and I may not need to," Katie said as she turned and headed toward the front of the office.

It was Wednesday, just after they had returned from lunch and she walked up front to look out the big picture window, facing the street. She got to the window as a little red pickup zipped by.

She had seen it plain as day. It was Nick. At least there wasn't another woman with him, it was his brother Why would he come home from college and not tell her? He hadn't called to tell her he was coming home. What would entice him to come home in the middle of the week? When she imagined another girl, she figured it would be someone from college, but maybe she was wrong, and there was someone here in town.

Katie, trying not to cry, said, "Maybe I should just drive out there and surprise him, and see what is going on." That seemed to get everyone's attention at work.

One of the men in her office tried to console her. "You'll only make things worse," he told her, "if you make waves."

He convinced her that Nick just needed to work on the barn or track. He then gave her a big project to work on and tried to get her mind on something different for the afternoon.

Margaret, a friend in the office decided she better call Nick and tell him that the worry of losing him was getting to be too much for Katie.

"Hello, Nick, Katie knows something is going on, and she is worrying herself sick. She saw you going through town," Margaret warned Nick.

"Thanks for calling Margaret, I appreciate it," Nick told her. He then decided he would meet Katie at five o'clock when she got off work. He would surprise her and take her out to eat. His dad had been telling him he was ignoring her too much. Nick knew the amount of work this project involved, and he was trying to meet his school requirements, work at the arena as much as possible, and struggle with the project at home too. He was tired, but still eager to finish his project, making it a big surprise for Katie.

April 23 was set for the wedding date. The spring planting season would go smoother for everyone, and the wedding would be over by the time it got into full swing. Although Nick would not quite be finished with school, it would be only a short time 'till graduation. Everything had to be planned around the planting or harvest season, and she could understand that, especially after working though several seasons with the family. There would not be time to work on a wedding during a busy season at the farm.

The way everyone was treating her, she felt that they only wanted her around for the work she could do. After all, she hadn't been out to the farm since harvest.

When she went out the back door at five o'clock she was very surprised to see Nick waiting for her. She was so delighted to see him. Nick hadn't really realized how upset she was about not seeing him. It was true he had been so preoccupied, but when he held her in his arms, he realized how much he had missed being with her every day.

They went out to eat and Katie was feeling much better. After the meal, they planned to go to the show. "Does this remind you of anything?" Nick asked Katie .

"Are you referring to our first date?"

"Yes, I am, I bet you didn't think I would remember."

"Well, the way it has been going lately, I was beginning to wonder if you even remembered me," Katie said. It came out a little more blunt than she really meant for it to sound.

"Oh, honey, I remember you! Don't worry, I remember. Didn't I propose to you one time?"

"What do you mean by that?"

"You'll see! Someday, you'll see. I remember you, without a doubt. I'm the guy who loves you!" Nick said.

"Well, sometimes you couldn't tell it by looking," The music began, the show commenced, and that was the end of the conversation.

Katie had no way of knowing how hard he had been working or how many hours he had been putting in. When he fell asleep at the movie, she was shattered. She was so mad! She could hardly sit and watch the rest of the show. He started to snore once and she elbowed him so hard he jumped. It didn't do any good, because he soon dropped his head and dozed off again. She would have loved to have gotten up and walked out, but they were in his truck and she had no way back to her car.

I have never been so mad in my life, she thought to herself. I can't believe this, we never spend time together and when we do, he falls asleep.

She woke him up when the movie was over and barely said a word to him as they drove back to her car. He could tell she was just a little disgusted with him, but he couldn't help falling asleep. And he couldn't or wouldn't let himself cave in now and tell her everything he had been doing. There were just certain things she wouldn't understand until this project was finished.

When they got back to her car she jumped out of his truck, slammed the door, and got in her vehicle. Nick decided that maybe it was more than a *little* disgusted. He got out of his truck and stood by her car until she finally rolled down her window. He could see the tears glistening in her eyes and spilling down her face.

"Katie, I'm sorry, I didn't mean to fall asleep. I couldn't help it." She didn't look too forgiving. She just glared at him.

"Please, Katie, give me another couple weeks," he said. "I love you, Katie."

"A couple of weeks, why is that? Do you need to break up with your girlfriend at school? Or maybe you are deciding which one of us you like the best. You never come home from school anymore. Then today you come home and don't tell me you are coming? What happened? Was the girlfriend tied up? I want to know what exactly is going on! I mean it, Nick!

I have never been this mad or hurt. I can't believe you would act this way! Shoot, your whole family must be in on it, too! Maybe mine too, for all I know. They never want me to come to their house either. Maybe your folks like the other girl better. Is she pretty? Does she like horses? You have exactly two weeks, Nick, and you better have your mind made up. Either me all the way, and we talk about a place to live when we get married, or we call the wedding off, and I never want to see you again. Right now, I would just love to move to a different city, get a job there, and be as far away from you as possible."

She was yelling so loud and sobbing so hard by this time that Nick wanted to take her in his arms, hold her, comfort her, help her to understand, and make her stop crying.

"Katie, honey, I love you," Nick said, but he didn't think she heard him. She rolled up the window as soon as she had finished yelling at him. The car was in gear and she was backing up!

As she backed out of the parking place he yelled, "There is no other girl, and I love you, Katie!"

She sped out of the parking lot behind her office and away she went, not looking back at him.

When she got home, she paced the floor for at least thirty minutes. The phone rang a couple times but she didn't answer it. She was sure it would be Nick and she didn't want to talk to him tonight or hear his flimsy excuses. She wanted to wait a few days, get herself together, and then have a good heart-to-heart talk with him.

After all, it was her heart that was hurting, she thought. She wanted to have a sincere discussion, when she wasn't so upset. As she said her prayers and snuggled down in her bed for the night, she couldn't help but wonder why Nick had asked for a couple more weeks.

Chapter 30

"What am I going to do?" Nick asked his mom the next morning at breakfast.

"I don't know what you mean, son? Do about what?" she asked as she continued to load the dishwasher.

"About Katie, mom. You know how much I love her, but I just can't handle much more. I'm so worn out and tired. I don't see much of her anymore, and she is getting really aggravated at me. Last night I tried to make it up to her by taking her out to eat and then to the show. However, I fell asleep at the show. When I took her back to her car, I was afraid she was going to dump me right there, on the parking lot.

"She actually told me as she was getting in the car that she was thinking of moving to another city, and that I would have to take a number and stand in line because I wasn't the only person who didn't love her anymore. She thinks her folks don't love her either. Katie said they acted like they didn't want her to come to their house anymore, and she is convinced you don't like her at all," Nick went on to tell his mom.

"Oh. my! Nick, I never thought about it getting to this

point. I figured she would feel a little neglected, but never thought it would go this far. That poor child, I can't imagine all the things she thinks about us all."

"Oh, mom, you haven't heard it all. She thinks I'm seeing someone else! I'm working as hard as I can to make all this come together. There just don't seem to be enough hours in the day, and then to top it all off, she thinks I'm seeing someone else," Nick told his mom.

"I wish we could help you more, son. You are beginning to look really worn out."

"Thanks, mom. You and dad have already done a lot. If you think I look bad, you should see Katie. She has lost so much weight, she is so thin. Mom, I wanted this to be such a wonderful project and it is taking a turn for the worse. I never dreamed it would consume my life and I wouldn't get to see Katie ."

"Okay, Nick. Here's what we are going to do. We may have to cut some of your wonderful project short, but that may be a good thing. She might like helping some, too. So I'm going to plan the biggest birthday party ever for her. She probably thinks we have forgotten all about her birthday. Since it's over the Thanksgiving weekend, we will tell her it is for her and your dad," Sue reached for a tablet of paper to begin making her list.

"But, mom, I can't get everything done that I wanted to have done before then."

"I know, Nick, but the main things will be done. Once she finds out what has been going on she will want to help with a lot of it. Besides, I feel sorry for her, and a little bit guilty, too. I should have called her more.

"Anna will be so relieved. She has missed doing things with Katie, and she will love helping with the party. Plus the girls will be so excited. They can help, too. I can't wait to call Anna and get started on it. We can't let Katie get completely sick. She is going to be a bride, remember?"

"Remember? Whose bride do you think she is going to be? That is, if she doesn't leave me before we are married," Nick said.

"Well, that is another reason to plan this party, to keep her from leaving you before you get the project done. Come on, Nick. Just get as much as you can done between now and the party, and that will be good enough. She will love you forever and ever for this present, I'm sure."

About that time Carl walked in. "What is your mom smiling about?" Carl asked Nick.

"Oh, I came in here telling her how depressed I was and crying on her shoulder, so she is planning a party. You know how she loves stuff like that," Nick told his dad.

"Planning a party? Who is it for, and when and where?" Carl asked.

"It is for Katie, for her birthday, and it is going to be down at the creek; and yes, I do love planning parties. I'm hoping it will lift all our spirits. I've got so many ideas spinning in my head, I need to get them jotted down before I forget," Sue told the guys.

"What about being all decorated for Christmas?" Carl asked.

Sue snickered "You might know that would be your main concern," Sue said.

"Well, I like Christmas and I thought you wanted the site decorated before she saw it," Carl said.

Nick put his head down. "I did, dad, but I think she will leave me before I could get that far along

"Sue you call Pam down at the flower shop and order the biggest and prettiest Christmas wreath. You know the kind of Christmas decorations that Katie liked the best. Tell her to make it the prettiest one Katie has ever seen!" Carl said.

"Good idea!" Sue had accomplished one thing at least. Both guys were smiling and throwing out Ideas faster than she could write them down.

She would call Anna later. She wanted to give her time to get the girls off to school. Anna would be full of suggestions and thrilled that this secret was about to be let out of the bag.

When she told Anna of the plans, she was excited and eager to help.

"Who is going to call Katie and tell her about the party?" Nick asked. I'm not sure she will answer my calls or talk to me. I'm going to have to get back to college. I have a class late this morning. In fact, I need to be leaving right now. I will be pushing it to get there in time as it is. Luckily there isn't as much traffic on the roads during the week."

"I'll call her at work and she will talk to me." Sue said.

Sue gave Katie a call at work, "Hello, Katie. I've just got a minute, got to go to the bank for Carl, but I wanted to tell you that Anna and I are planning a party for you and Carl on the Friday after Thanksgiving and we will be looking forward to seeing you then. Don't make any other plans."

"Okay, I guess," Katie said.

"Well, I must go, bye-bye, hon, and we love you," Sue said.

"Now that was short and sweet," Nick said when his mother hung up the phone.

"Yeah, how come you are going to the bank for me?" Carl asked.

"Well, I'm like everyone else, I'm afraid to talk to her

194

very long. I'm afraid I'll spill the beans. I just told her I was going to the bank. I said what needed to be said and she agreed. I got the job done. Now, you need to be going, don't drive too fast, be careful. We love you, son."

Katie looked at one of her friends and said, "Now, that was unusual."

"Who was it? You didn't talk long," Margaret said.

"It was Nick's mom. She says they are going to have a birthday party for me and Nick's dad the day after Thanksgiving. I would say she doesn't know about the blow-up last night, but then it was funny because she told me she loved me at the end of the conversation. But she sure was in a hurry."

Chapter 31

Nick called her Friday at work and said, "Honey, I'm so sorry but something came up and I have a chance to work here at the college, I just can't make it home this weekend,. I'd really love to, but I can't pass up this opportunity. Remember I love you."

He sounded sad that he wasn't coming, and yet if he had made the trip home for the weekend, he probably wouldn't have spent much time with her anyway. She knew he would have been busy working on the barn to start his horse operation. It consumed his time completely and the new horse business was all that was on his mind. She knew for sure that *she* wasn't consuming too much of his time.

What she couldn't understand was why she was never included. If this were going to be *their* family business, why did Nick repeatedly ignore her? There always seemed to be some flimsy reason why she shouldn't come out to the site.

She was already tired of the word "site." One evening during one of the short visits Nick allowed them on the phone, she mentioned, "You know, Nick, I haven't seen the 'site' since you started work on it. I'd love to see how you are coming along."

After all the talk of how they were working on the site and the long hours they were putting in, he then said, "Oh, Katie. It isn't much yet. You need to wait awhile to come out and then you can really see what we have done. Just a lot of dirt work so far. You would just have to stand around and watch if you were there."

They still hadn't had a discussion about the night they went to the show. No talk of a house, no apology from either of them, and this bothered Katie . She knew she had behaved badly and she wanted to tell Nick why she felt the way she did. Could things ever be as they were before? They both acted as though the episode had never happened. She was definitely beginning to wonder about their future together. She loved him so, but the closeness between them seemed strained.

Nick went on to say, "There will be plenty for you to do later."

"So, as usual, when the hard work starts, you'll be sure I'm there. I think I need to go. Sounds like someone drove up in my driveway," she lied.

She hadn't meant for that to come out of her mouth and she wished she could take it back, but that was the way she felt at the moment. "You and your big mouth," she said aloud to herself as she sat down on the couch and began to weep.

Chapter 32

Saturday morning, she could sleep late, and here it was five o'clock and she was wide awake. She had already tossed and turned for an hour; she decided she would just get up. When she looked outside, the dawn was giving way to a cloudy dreary -looking morning.

She was restless. She couldn't seem to sit still. She tried to clean house but soon lost interest. Working on the quilt did not hold her attention for long. After coffee and a shower, she decided that she would drive to the college and surprise Nick.

A drive down there would be nice and she hadn't been to the college in quite awhile. She would be able to watch the event that was going on today. It must be an event of some magnitude, and they thought they needed some extra people, since they had asked him to stay and help.

When he had called last night to say he wouldn't be able to come home as planned, she was so disappointed that she had failed to ask what was going on at the coliseum. She hadn't seen Nick near as often as she would have liked in the past few weeks, and was hoping that this weekend might be different.

Katie was ashamed of herself, too. She knew that

on the few times she did see him, she had been rather sarcastic. Why would he want to see her? Every time they were together she continued to harp on the house. She promised herself that today she would make sure she didn't bring up the house. Hopefully, they would have a fun day, and it would be like old times. She wanted lots of laughter.

I'll try my grandma's approach, she thought. She wore the outfit that Nick had bragged on the last time she wore it, and she put on the boots he had given her recently. In addition, of course, like most men, Nick loved her hair down, so she took special pains in fixing it just as he would like. A twirl in front of the mirror just before she headed out the door proved that she did look nice. She hoped Nick would think so, and be proud of her when he saw her.

Of course, in the back of her mind she was thinking, a surprise element might be good if there was another girl hanging around.

She got there around twelve o'clock and went down to the stalls where she thought she would find him. There were a couple familiar faces and she started asking about Nick. No one had seen him that morning. One guy told her that he thought for sure he was going home for the weekend. Then he asked, "Do you own one of the horses he has been working with this past week?"

"No, I don't own any horses. I'm his fiancée."

"Uh-oh!" the young man said.

"What do you mean uh-oh?" Katie asked.

"Well, uh, now, you know, I don't know for sure if he went home. Let me help you see if we can find him. He may be here," the guy said.

"I think you have already done enough," Katie said. She could tell he knew more than he was saying, and he knew he shouldn't have told her that Nick had gone home.

Even some of the people down here knew something was going on.

She started to walk off, then turned around and went back to him. "Would you just tell me the truth. Does he have another girl on the side? No one will tell me anything, but something is up, I can tell."

"I don't know anything, Katie. I really don't, but I'll take you out for lunch if you'll go. You can cry on my shoulder, honey. I know if I had a gal as pretty as you, I sure wouldn't be looking for another one."

"How did you know my name," Katie asked.

"Well, Nick always talks about you," he said.

"Does he ever mention any other girls' names?"

"No, I don't think so. Come on let me buy you lunch. Let's run up here to the place on Hwy 13 and I'll buy you a sandwich, we could talk and maybe you would feel better," he said as he laid his hand on her shoulder.

Katie hesitated for a few seconds, thinking, this would really get to Nick if he found out I had lunch with someone else, and this guy sounds caring. I need to talk to someone.

About that time he slipped his arm down around her waist and started walking and pulling her along. "Come on, doll. You will feel better after lunch. I'll hold your hand while you tell me the whole story."

She decided she didn't want to be in a car with this guy by herself. She started to pull away and told him she needed to check with a few other people.

As she tried to pull away, he grabbed her by the arm and held on tight.

"You are hurting me. Let go!" she said.

"I'm not hurting you. Come on and have a bite to eat with me and then we will go have some fun," he said.

From somewhere behind her, Katie heard a deep voice.

"She doesn't look interested in going to grab a bite with you, or anything else for that matter. Let her go, Derrick," Lucas said.

"What have you got to say about this? It is none of your business, Lucas," Derrick said.

"Well, Derrick, I'm making it my business. I think Nick would want me to step in, and since I'm about 150 pounds bigger than you and so is John, I'd suggest you let go of the girl."

"What has John got to do with what is going on here?" Derrick asked.

"Well, he is peeping around the corner behind you, just waiting for me to give him the nod," Lucas replied.

John popped around the corner about that time. "Come on Lucas, let's practice a little tackle football on the little jerk," John said. "Let me go first."

"What is she to you?" Derrick asked Lucas.

"Besides being my roommate's girlfriend, she is just a nice girl that doesn't want to go with you," Lucas said.

"If I let her go will you guys let me go?"

"You got a fifty-fifty chance, and if you don't let her go right now, there is a hundred percent chance you are going to get hurt," Lucas said.

"Ok, I'll leave." He started backing up. "Just don't hurt me. You guys are bigger than me. It wouldn't be a fair fight."

"And do you think you making Katie go with you would have been fair?" John asked.

Lucas grabbed him by the shirt and brought him up to his size. Look, I had better never hear of you harassing Katie, or any other girl for that matter. If I do, I guarantee you will regret it. Just because you think you are so good looking and the girls fall all over you, you can bully any of them around. Well, that's not the way it is, and you are going to have to learn the rules," Lucas said, as he tossed him in the direction of the end of the barn.

Katie was trying desperately not to cry. "Thank you both so much. You know, when he first mentioned going to grab a bite to eat, I almost said yes. Then he had his arm around me so tight... I don't even want to think about what might have happened. I was so glad to hear your voice,"

"We'll take care of you. Now what are you doing down here?" Lucas asked.

"Nick said he was working down here today, so I thought I would surprise him," Katie said.

"Uh-oh," John said.

"That is exactly what Derrick said before he got his hands on me, when I asked where Nick was," Katie said.

"Well, he just isn't here, Katie. That is all I meant," Lucas said.

"Just where is he? I think you know. In fact, I think John here knows, Derrick probably knows, too. I'm the only one who doesn't know. I'm supposed to marry this jerk and I can't find out what is going on. Come on, Lucas, spill your guts. You know something and I want to hear it.

"Even if there is another girl, I want to know about it," she said as her voice started to crack, With that, she stomped her foot and the tears started to flow.

"Oh, now, Katie , don't cry on me," Lucas said, as he gently put his arm around her. "I'm just not good at this, not good at it at all. I'm just a big old farm boy playing football to get through school, and I'm not good at consoling girls, and all that. How about you, John?"

"Me neither, no, not me. Come on, Katie. We can save you from some guy but don't cry on us," John said.

Katie had to smile; these two big guys were intimidated with a few tears. "I can't help it, I'm sorry, but I love Nick so much and I think he has found a new girl. Maybe I'll just have you guys beat her up, and him, too. Come to think of it."

"Now, Katie. Whoa! Hold on! Trust me here. Nick does not have another girl. That would never happen. He loves you, little girl." Moreover, she did look little standing by Lucas.

"Well, what am I supposed to think? This is ridiculous, Lucas. Something is going on. He is never where he says he's going to be, and he never wants to see me anymore," Katie said.

"Nothing is going on. You just have to trust us on this one," John said. "Be patient. I know it is hard, but this time you have to be a little tolerant."

"If I hear that again I'll scream. That is what everyone says. Then the other day Nick says 'Oh, honey, give me a break, I just need a little time.' Time, he needs time, time for what, so he can break up with his girlfriend! On the other hand, is he going to break up with me? Then he tells me he is working, so I drive several hours down here and he isn't here. Tell me what you would think. *Trust me* on this one. I'm going back to his house, give him back this ring, and give him a piece of my mind. I have had it!"

"You can't do that, Katie," Lucas said. "Come on, John, help me out here. Now, Katie, we three are going to make a deal. We didn't see you and you haven't seen us. You are going to calm down and drive home very carefully. That is, to your house, not to Nick's or anyplace else."

"Look at this calendar," John said as he pointed to one hanging on the wall. He took out his pen and circled the Monday after Thanksgiving. "Make a deal with ya. If you still want us to on this day, you let us know, and we will beat him up for you. Just say the word, but you have to calm down and wait until this Monday. My dad always said not to make any snap decisions when you are mad. However, if you cool down and then you still want us to whip him, we will do it here. I'm free that day," he said, flashing a sexy smile. "How about you, Lucas? Do you think you would have time to beat up Nick?"

"He's right, you just let us know what you need, three broken bones or two pints of blood on the floor, two black eyes, you just tell us," Lucas agreed.

"I think you guys are nuts but I thank you for saving me and for making me smile. I'll be talking to you about Monday," and she smiled back at them. "I'm going home now and stay there, I promise. If I would see Nick, I'd tell him off, I know I would.

I'll wait, like you said, but I am not waiting any longer. If nothing changes by then, I am calling off the wedding. Right now, I feel like I never want to see him again. I can't believe I said that. I love him so much, and never want to see him again. That is strange, but I'll do as you said, and I never saw either of you today. I haven't been here!"

With that little speech said, she turned and walked out to the parking lot, got in her car, and drove off.

Lucas and John just looked at each other. They didn't know if they should mention the incident to Nick or not. "We need to discuss this and decide what the best thing to do would be," John said.

Chapter 33

Katie was shaking. She was so upset that she had driven all the way down to the coliseum and Nick wasn't there. She would spend almost all day on the road and not get to see Nick at all. He had lied to her. There was no other way to look at it. He had lied! He told her he was staying at the college this weekend for some big event. Ha! She was the only car on the parking lot. He wasn't there and there was no event this morning.

Lucas and John were in on some secret. She had no idea what it was, but there was something going on. Why did they want her to wait to tell Nick off? Something was up and they knew about it. She decided that she would do as they asked.

In her wildest imagination, she couldn't imagine anything being worth all the anguish she had gone through. There had to be another girl, Katie decided. As she left, she promised them she would wait the two weeks and she would keep her word, although she felt Nick had not kept his word to her.

These thoughts were whirling through her mind. She had no idea what was going on, but today's events had taken its toll on her. She felt drained and exhausted, almost too tired to drive home. Disappointed and weary she felt like a limp rag. But, it had been her choice to come down here to surprise him and her idea had backfired. Now she had to make the long trip back home.

She stopped for gas and a snack, before getting on the interstate, thinking that maybe some chocolate would revive and refresh her. As she went in to pay for the gas, she noticed some young guy leaning on the counter, flirting with the cashier. They were the only people in the little mart. She went on to the bathroom and then got her cappuccino and snack, hoping the guy would leave and she wouldn't have to interrupt their conversation.

As she walked up to the counter to pay for the gas and snacks, she came face-to-face with the young man. She gasped! "Oh, no!"

"Where are your body guards now, Katie?" Derrick asked.

She took a deep breath, laid her items on the counter and tried to ignore him. In the back of her mind she thought, what am I going to do? There were no other people on the lot or in the store. The girl behind the counter still had her eyes on Derrick, and Katie could tell she had a crush on him and would not be any help all. She took Katie's money and gave back her change.

The phone rang at that time and she went off to take care of the caller. Judging from this end of the conversation, Katie thought it sounded as if it was a friend, calling to visit.

"Oh, great!" Katie said under her breath.

She was afraid Derrick would follow her out to her truck. At this point, she didn't know what else to do but try her best to get in her truck and get the doors locked.

Unfortunately, she was right. When she opened the

door and started outside, he walked out with her. She was terrified.

He managed to get between her and her truck. She looked back to the station window, but the cashier had turned her back.

"What are you going to do now, sweetie? Let's finish what we started before we were so rudely interrupted earlier today. What do you think about that idea?" He leaned back against her truck door and pulled her over to him, standing with both arms around her.

She was still holding her purchases and all the while thinking of what her next move would be. First she had to get him away from her door. She didn't want to make him mad right off. She wanted to handle this in a calm manner if possible.

"No, I am not going with you, not now or ever! Just leave me alone, Derrick. Let me go my way and I won't tell Lucas that you bothered me again. Let go of me, Derrick."

"You don't seem to be in control right now. There doesn't seem to be a lot of people around here at the moment."

What is wrong with me? Why didn't I pick the busier station, she thought. More people would have been a plus at this moment. Where were all the customers?

"Now relax, Katie. Your boyfriend doesn't seem to be paying attention to you and he lied to you about where he was going to be, so why not go out with me for a fun evening? We'll go get something to eat and talk for a while. I'm not going to hurt you. I just want to go out with a good-looking gal and have some fun.

"I don't want to go anyplace with you, Derrick, I want to get in my truck and leave. Why won't you leave me alone? Go back in and talk to the cashier, she seemed interested."

"Oh, honey, she is more than interested. I'm coming

back at 11:30 to pick her up when she gets off and show her a real good time. You're first though, Katie. Just get in my truck and go peacefully, and no one gets hurt. I know just the place to go and no one will bother us."

Derrick took Katie by the arm and started guiding her to his truck. She was now close to the panic stage. Don't let him get you close to his truck, she told herself. She didn't know what she was going to do yet, but getting in the truck with this jerk was not one of the choices. Stop trembling, she thought.

"Well, you may be right. That would show him, wouldn't it? You buying the food?"

"Sure, I'll buy anything you want," he said, a little more than surprised at her change of attitude.

"A good steak dinner would be nice. I'm really hungry. Then we could go have some real fun," Katie said, in her best attempt to sound sexy.

"Now you're talkin', girl. Let's go," Derrick said.

"You know a good romp with you would really make Nick jealous when he finds out about it. I can't wait to tell him myself and see the look on his face. You better make this worth my while," she said and looked up at Derrick, and batting her eyes a few times.

"Oh, I will, I promise you. Come on, let's go."

He was very close and had his arm around her very tightly, as he walked her toward his truck.

"Well, hon," and she stopped, "I need to get my purse out of my truck I just took my credit card in the station with me. I need to move it out of the way, too." She gave him a little peck on the cheek and sort of rubbed up against him in as sexual a manner as she knew how, and said, "Just give me a second and I'll be ready to go. I think you are right. This is going to be fun. I'll just show Nick a thing or two; he can't lie to me and get by with it. When he finds out I've had some fun with you, then he will be the one hurting inside."

"And you will have fun with me, I can guarantee it. I can't wait to see your face."

"And I can't wait to see yours!" Katie said.

Still clutching the large cappuccino she had just purchased, she eased her hand up to the top of the cup and with one finger raised the plastic lid on one side.

"You aren't going to try anything and slip off on me are you?"

"Not now," she whispered, he was still so close to her. "I tell you what, let's go to your little secluded place first and then go eat. I don't think I can wait much longer."

"All right!" He let go of her for a second to clap his hands and she moved closer to her little pickup.

"I'll move my pickup over there." She tossed her snacks in the truck, but she was still clutching the cappuccino, very carefully. Trying not to rush and draw attention to herself, she got in the truck but he was too quick. He grabbed the door before she could slam it shut. Quick as lightning, she threw the entire cappuccino at his face, but he jerked her arm, and hot liquid hit his body just below the waist. Still he didn't turn loose of her arm.

She tried to slam the door but his arm was in it, which made him even madder. He grabbed her out of the truck in one quick motion, and threw a punch in her direction. She was already shifting her body to kick him. As she made this move, luckily, she moved her head to the side.

He missed her face by a fraction of an inch but hit the cab of Katie's truck full force with his fist. Lucky for Katie, he didn't see her leg coming. She hit her target perfectly with the sharp toe of her cowboy boot.

He dropped to the parking lot on his knees. Her

surprise kick had rendered him helpless for the moment. It had taken him totally off guard.

Katie wasted no time jumping in her truck, slamming the door, and hitting the lock button. She squealed her tires as she left the parking lot, and caught a glimpse of the cashier stretching her neck to look out the window. When she looked in her mirror, Derrick was still on the parking lot, rocking back and forth in pain.

She thought of the poor gal behind the counter, but sort of smiled as she thought of Derrick. He would probably be out of business for a few hours and wouldn't be able to rape the gal when she got off work. Of course, that girl had seemed much more willing to go with Derrick, and was smart enough to know what would take place. She was much more interested than Katie had been.

Katie's heart was racing as she realized she had escaped! She grabbed a Kleenex and wiped her mouth. It felt dirty from kissing him on the cheek, but that was the only way she could get closer to her truck. Would he follow her? That was her biggest fear. Was he able to follow her? She hurried and got back into the main flow of traffic as soon as possible to try to lose him. She tried to look back but she couldn't see clearly. She didn't think his truck was moving yet, but she wasn't sure.

Chapter 34

I hope there are no troopers out this afternoon, she thought, as she sped away from the gas station. Of course, if one would have driven up as she was being pressured to get in his truck, she would have been thankful.

She wanted to get away from Derrick so he wouldn't follow her. There was so much traffic at the intersection that she was in hopes of getting lost in the crowd. Once she was on the interstate headed north, she still couldn't relax. She was gripping the steering wheel so hard her knuckles were white.

She slowed and let a few trucks pass her so she could see what the traffic looked like behind them. There were only a couple of small cars as far back as she could see. If he was following her, she was sure he would be in sight.

After a couple deep breaths, she tried hard to breathe more regularly. Then she released the steering wheel with one hand, and flexed her fingers back and forth a few times. Her hands were cramping she had been gripping the wheel so hard.

I wish I hadn't had to waste my cappuccino on that twit, she thought to herself. But she had to smile when she remembered the surprised look on his face, both when he got the cappuccino on the pants and when the cowboy boot had hit its target. She hated to think what would have happened to her if she had not gotten away from him.

She should probably tell Lucas what happened, but she didn't want Lucas to get himself in trouble. On the other hand, she didn't want some other young girl to be victimized by this jerk who thought he could do anything he wanted where girls were concerned.

Should she stop again? Her throat was so dry, but she was still shaken from her last episode. She finally decided that she would stop at the next exit and buy another cappuccino, hopefully she wouldn't have to dump it in someone's face, or any other place. Very alert and cautiously she pulled over at a very busy station, got her drink, and hurried back to the truck, and was again on her way.

She was so glad to be home. She hurried in the house and locked the door behind her. It was a relief to be in her own home and she couldn't wait to take a shower and get to bed. After putting on her favorite pajamas, she covered up and cried herself to sleep.

Sunday she stayed at home, and when Nick and her mother called, she just told them she didn't feel like getting out and maybe they should neither one come over since she might have something catching. It seemed to her that they both almost sounded delighted that she was under the weather. Was that her imagination, or were they relieved that they didn't have to mess with her today? She thought she even heard a sigh of relief from her mom.

When Nick had called that morning, she cut him off, saying she needed to lay back down. She didn't ask how the event went yesterday at the arena; she didn't want to hear his lies. What was she to think? Most of the day was spent lounging around and feeling sorry for herself.

About 6 o'clock there was a faint knock at the door. She was so surprised when she answered the door and found Nick standing there with a small crock-pot in his hand. "May I come in?" he asked.

"Sure. But if you get something, don't blame me."

She did look bad, Nick thought, but he couldn't help but think she looked more like she had been crying and not sick.

"Are you all right?"

"I've been better. I've probably looked better, too. Sorry," she said as she tried to smooth her hair. She was ashamed of how she looked.

"That's okay. I love you no matter how you look."

"Yeah, right."

"Do you want to sit down?"

"Why don't you let me heat up this stew? I'd love to say I made it myself, but mom really did. I'm on my way back to school, but wanted to run by and drop this off. I wanted to see how you were doing."

"Aren't you afraid of catching something? I don't want to keep you from going back to school."

"It is okay Katie. I've got time. What's the problem?"

"What does it really matter?"

"Katie, it does matter. I don't want you sick and I don't want you in this kind of mood."

"I can't help it. That is just the way I feel right now! I can heat up the stew, you can go on back if you want." She wanted him to stay and baby her, maybe take her in his arms, but she had pushed him away.

"Are you sure? What do you really want, Katie?"

She lost the battle of holding back the tears at that point. He did put his arms around her and held her. They walked over to the couch and he held her and let her cry. There seemed to be no stopping. How could she explain what was wrong, as she had promised Lucas and John that she wouldn't tell she had been down there.

As long as he had his arms around her she felt so protected and safe. She didn't want him to take them away. Nick was baffled. He had no idea what could be upsetting her to this point, and she didn't seem to be giving him any explanation.

Chapter 35

Thanksgiving morning finally arrived. Nick was supposed to come out to the house and pick her up and they were going to her folks house for a big dinner. But early that morning, her mom called and said that they were having trouble with the stove, the oven didn't want to heat up, so Dad had suggested that he take them out for turkey and dressing.

She couldn't believe it. They had never gone out to eat on Thanksgiving, but that was what her dad wanted to do. Katie begged them to bring the turkey up to her house and cook it, but they wouldn't hear of it.

So for Thanksgiving dinner they went out to eat. It was very good but the dressing couldn't compare to her mother's. They had a good meal and were glad to leave the cleanup to someone else.

After dinner they drove out to look at the big lake close by. It was so low it had made the news. It was the water source for several towns and with it being so very low it was a major concern for everyone. It was the lowest the lake had been since it was built in the 1960s.

Katie asked Nick what his folks were doing and he said that they had a few things to do yet to get ready for the birthday party tomorrow. It wasn't going to be anything fancy, but his mom was cooking a big supper for them all.

"Can we go out and help her?" Katie asked. He was quick to tell her that it was all under control. Anna was coming over to help when she got back from Thanksgiving dinner at her folks' house, so she didn't need to drive out.

That didn't surprise her. She just more or less offered to see what the excuse would be. She knew there would be one.

As the day was winding down, and Nick had gone home, she settled down to work on her quilt. It had been a little strange, but still nice, in fact a really nice day, and she couldn't count the times that Nick had told her he loved her. He had said that tomorrow might prove to be busy, and he just wanted her to know how much he loved her.

When he left he had kissed her so tenderly, she enjoyed just sitting there thinking about the kiss. It made goose pimples go up and down her spine. How wonderful it would be to be married to this man.

He had said, "Katie, I'll be after you at noon tomorrow. Twelve o'clock sharp. Don't be late, and don't make me wait. I love you."

Why was he all of a sudden telling her how much he loved her after putting her through torture all those weeks? She still couldn't figure out what was going on. If things didn't change and if everyone didn't start treating her differently, she might still call off the wedding.

Chapter 36

Katie woke early. Today would be a day to remember. By the end of the day, she was determined to have some answers. She wanted answers as to why everyone was treating her the way they had been, and answers to questions about a house for them to live in. If no one wanted to discuss a house, then maybe there would be no need for one in the future. Nick could just have the barn and his horses to himself.

She had a feeling the day would hold some surprises, and felt that by the end of the day she would know for sure if she was going to marry into this family.

After she got ready for the party, she sat down to wait for the appointed hour. As she was waiting she put a few stitches in the quilt. She couldn't believe it, but she was sewing in the last section of the Grandmother's Flower Garden that her grandmother had started so many long years ago.

How ironic, the day that she might call off the wedding and she finished putting the quilt together. She should be so happy, but she didn't know if she was going to be happy or sad when this day was over. She was proud of the quilt top and she would decide what to do about actually quilting it herself after today.

She spread out the quilt top on her bed and admired it. She was so proud of it and all the memories it held. She was also proud of the work she had done. It lay so nice and she could almost imagine how it would look all puffy and quilted.

Chapter 37

She was just folding up the quilt as Nick drove up. He honked, which he never did when he came to her house. He honked, jumped out of the truck and came to the door, and nearly drug her out to the truck.

She barely had time to grab her jacket and purse. They started to leave, then he pulled back in her drive and said, "You better get a heavier coat and some old shoes or boots. And, hey, did you say you finished the quilt? Bring that along, too. Mom will like seeing it."

"What are we going to do that I need boots and a big coat?" she asked.

"No questions today, sweetheart, no questions. You ain't seen nothing yet," he said.

She wondered if they were going to have the party in the mud. What on earth was going on here? She had just bought those new tennis shoes and he wanted her to wear boots. Probably going to do some more work, that was when they wanted her around she had decided.

It was starting to snow. It made her think of the first time they had actually talked.

She couldn't help but notice Nick's smile today. He just beamed. She hadn't seen that smile in so long. It felt like ages since they had really spent quality time together, and she missed his lighthearted teasing and his laugh. He just kept looking over at her and smiling, and at one point he did say, "I sure hope you like your birthday present."

When they got to the corner to turn to go to Nick's family farm, his dad's four-wheel-drive truck was parked there. Nick pulled up and told her to switch trucks and put on her boots and heavy coat.

She started to open her mouth to ask why, but he said, "Remember, no questions today, no, not one."

Well, she was pretty sure she had this figured out. He had bought her a horse. She hoped it was a black and white paint horse, as she liked those best. Maybe this was his way of showing her how they were going to start their operation.

When they both got in his dad's truck, Nick pulled out a nice clean cloth and told her she would have to be blindfolded from this point on. She couldn't believe this, but from the looks of the cloth and the fresh smell, she could tell that his mother had furnished it, and she must be in on this masquerade.

He blindfolded her and tied it plenty tight so that he was sure she couldn't see. Good thing it wasn't around her neck or she wouldn't be able to breathe either.

"I love you so much, Katie , I hope you will always remember today and know how much I love you," Nick said.

"Oh, yeah, I can tell, are you going to gag me, too?" Katie asked.

"No, that comes later, if you ask any more questions," Nick said.

Then Nick did something exceedingly strange, he did about four donuts in the middle of the road. When they took off, she had no idea really which way they were going, and just in case she did know, Nick would stop and do a donut or two at every wide place in the road.

He kept asking her if she could see, and she assured him she couldn't. "Nick, I have no idea where we are but if you do many more donuts, I'm going to throw up in your dad's truck. I'm really getting carsick."

"Sorry, I forgot about that problem. It's not much farther," he promised her. With that, he went on down the road, whistling his favorite tune.

Whatever he had up his sleeve, Katie didn't know for sure, but she knew he was pretty proud of himself. He had his arm around her and he was holding her so tight. It felt so good, and it had been so long since he had shown her any attention at all.

They slowed down and made one last turn. It was rough riding then, but Nick told her that this would smooth out with a few more loads of gravel. They must be going out to the new barn she figured, but knew there was no use in asking questions.

The truck came to a stop and he got out, telling her to sit still until he came around to her side. He opened the door and carefully helped her down. He held onto her arm and they walked slowly through some place that was rough. She had no idea where they were, but it was very quiet, almost eerily so, she thought. If there would have been a horse or two around she could have heard them breathing or walking.

Nick then stopped walking, turned her toward him and kissed her. All of a sudden, there was clapping and cheering and everyone was singing Happy Birthday.

He said, "Are you ready for the biggest surprise in your life?"

"Please get this blindfold off me, I can't stand this. Who all is here? Where are we? What is going on?"

Nick loved this far too much, he just calmly said, "Didn't I tell you, no questions?"

By this time she was trying to get the blindfold off her eyes herself. He put her hands down and proceeded to untie the cloth very slowly. When it fell to the ground, her mouth flew open and she gasped for air. She screamed. She just knew she couldn't breathe. It was unbelievable. It couldn't be true. Her knees were going weak and the world was spinning. She reached out for Nick, but he had moved. Luckily he turned and grabbed her just before she hit the ground. She woke up hearing him tell her to breathe, take deep breaths.

She was just so weak and the shock of what he revealed was almost too much. She sat on the cold ground with his arm around her and just stared. Could this really be true? There, right before her eyes stood her grandpa's house. She couldn't believe it.

All his family was on the front porch with a big pitcher full of lemonade, one of those big glass pitchers that was always used for Kool-Aid. Her folks were there, too, some of the people she worked with, and a few people she had never seen before. They were all sitting on the front porch with a glass of iced lemonade in the snowfall. These people really were nuts.

The house was nestled perfectly in the trees, and the porch banister was repaired and painted, just like grandpa had made it originally. Her dad must have been in charge of that. It even had the trellis at the end of the porch like it was when she was a little girl, and there was a new swing hanging on one end of the porch.

The house was all painted white and there was a beautiful wreath hung on the front door. That had to be compliments of Carl, since it was his tradition to put up Christmas decorations on the day after Thanksgiving.

"Now," she said, "Can I ask about ten thousand questions, like how did you do this? What does the inside look like? Who are some of these people, and why the lemonade?"

Everyone just burst out laughing, and she laughed along with them, she said she wished she had a picture of them all sitting on her front porch with lemonade in the snow storm. So her dad came off the porch and took some pictures. He had been taking pictures of the surprised look on Katie's face since Nick removed the blindfold.

Nick told her that he remembered how she had once said, that the porch just looked like it was built for drinking lemonade.

He finally asked if she could get up. He helped her up on the front porch and they went in the beautiful home. Not a lot had been done to the inside, he told her he wanted to let her do the decorating, and he was just in charge of getting it there.

She couldn't believe she had doubted this man. He had loved her so much that he had moved her grandpa's house up close to the horse operation.

He began to explain a few things, and several things were falling into place now. That was the reason she wasn't allowed to come to the farm or go to her folks'. She would have noticed the house being gone on her folks' road and although the house was a little off the road here, she would have wondered why the new road was being built and why the trees had been cut.

Nick told her to come and look out the back, through the dining room window. Katie was amazed to see the little creek running across her backyard, and the water trickling over the smaller sandstone pebbles. From out front she hadn't realized how close the house was to the big sandstone rock that they had sat on when he proposed.

The house really looked like it needed a good cleaning inside, but Nick had the outside painted, shined and polished. Some of the windows were repaired, and he told her he was ready to help her start cleaning and remodeling the inside. Nearly everyone there said they were eager to help.

Anna hugged her and hugged her. She told her that she was scared to call her because she was afraid she would give away the surprise. Nick had threatened anyone who let the cat out of the bag, so Anna and the girls had just stayed away from Katie altogether. Katie was so relieved; she had really missed Anna and the girls.

Katie whispered to Nick, asking who the two guys were who were standing off to the side, and Nick took her over to introduce her to the movers. They, too, were in on the surprise, and they said they wanted to see the look on her face when she saw the house.

It seemed as though everyone knew. The people she worked with were all in on it, and they said they were glad it was over. Everyone had been worried they would let the secret out.

They had set up tables in the dining room and everyone had brought food. Katie didn't think she had ever seen so much food.

The birthday cake Sue made was in the shape of the house. It was beautiful, Katie hated to cut it, but with a little coaxing, she dove into a big piece of it herself.

Then it was time to open birthday presents and every one of them was something for the house. It was more like a wedding shower. Katie loved everything. The last present was a very small box wrapped beautifully with quilt wrapping paper, Katie noticed. Inside the box was a handwritten note, which said, "Dear Katie, Nick tells me you have been piecing a quilt that was your grandmother's.

As my gift to you, I would like to quilt it for you when you finish. Love, Aunt Barb."

Tears came to Katie's eyes as she explained that she had just completed the piecing that morning. Nick's aunt told her to bring it over to the house next time she was over at Nick's.

Nick's mom spoke up and said, "She will be back soon, and often. We hated keeping you away, but Nick said this had to be a surprise."

"I'll get you the quilt. It is in the truck," Nick said. He was off to get the quilt top. When he brought it back and spread it out, everyone loved it. They bragged on the old fabrics in the quilt, talking about how new the old fabrics looked, and what a nice job Katie had done.

The afternoon ended too soon and people started leaving. Katie didn't want the day to end. What a wonderful day. How thankful to God she was that she had such a loving future husband and family.

She hugged everyone and thanked them all. Nick and Katie stood on the front porch arm in arm and waved to them all, calling out, "Thank you, and come back."

Chapter 38

After everyone had left, Katie hugged Nick, kissed him, and told him she had no idea how he had pulled this off but she was thrilled. Of course, she loved the house and the challenge of fixing it up, She couldn't wait to get started.

She then slugged him in the arm, pointed her finger in his face, and said, "Nick, don't you ever try anything like that again without telling me. This has been the most horrible last two months." By this time, she was sobbing again, "I thought no one at all loved me anymore. But I love you for doing this; you never cease to amaze me.

"When can we start cleaning and painting on the house? I can't wait. I don't want to leave here, and I don't want this day to end," she told Nick.

They both knew there was a lot more work to be done before they could live there, and it would take a lot of time and elbow grease.

Just as the patchwork quilt had been pieced together, so had small pieces of their lives.

Nick said, "I'm going to put up the mailbox first thing tomorrow. It was my favorite gift. It has our name on it.

"MR. AND MRS. HOOGERHYDE."

LaVergne, TN USA
19 March 2011
220761LV00001B/2/P